101 Tips
for a
Happy Marriage

101 Tips for a Happy Marriage

Ayatullāh Sayyid Ali Khamenei

﴿وَمِنْ آيَاتِهِ أَنْ خَلَقَ لَكُم مِّنْ أَنفُسِكُمْ أَزْوَاجًا لِّتَسْكُنُوا إِلَيْهَا وَجَعَلَ بَيْنَكُم مَّوَدَّةً وَرَحْمَةً إِنَّ فِي ذَٰلِكَ لَآيَاتٍ لِّقَوْمٍ يَتَفَكَّرُونَ﴾

101 Tips for a Happy Marriage

Terms of Respect

The following Arabic phrases have been used throughout this book in their respective places to show the reverence which the noble personalities deserve.

Used for Allāh (God) meaning:
Exalted and Sublime (Perfect) is He

Used for Prophet Muḥammad meaning:
Blessings from Allāh be upon him and his family

Used for a man of high status (singular) meaning:
Peace be upon him

Used for woman of a high status (singular) meaning:
Peace be upon her

Used for men/women of a high status (dual) meaning:
Peace be upon them both

Used for men and/or women of a high status (plural) meaning:
Peace be upon them all

Used for a deceased scholar meaning:
May his resting [burial] place remain pure

Copyright

Copyright © 2022 al-Burāq Publications.

All rights reserved. No part of this publication may be reproduced, distributed, or transmitted in any form or by any means, including photocopying, recording, or other electronic or mechanical methods, without the prior written permission of the publisher, except in the case of brief quotations embodied in critical reviews and certain other noncommercial uses permitted by copyright law. For permission requests, write to the publisher, addressed "Attention: Permissions [101 Tips for a Happy Marriage]," at the email address below.

ISBN: 978-1-956276-11-4.

Translated and annotated by al-Burāq Publications. Where needed, context and transliterations were added.

Printed and published by al-Burāq Publications.

Ordering Information

We offer discounts and promotions for wholesale purchases and for non-profit organizations, libraries, and other educational institutions. Contact us at the email below for further information.

www.al-Buraq.org
publications@al-Buraq.org

First edition | January 2022

Dedication

The publication of this book was made possible through the generous support of our donors.

Please recite *Sūrah al-Fātiha* and ask Allāh for the Divine reward (*thawāb*) to be conferred upon the donors and also the souls of all the deceased in whose memory their loved ones have contributed graciously towards the publication of *101 Tips for a Happy Marriage*.

We begin by giving all praise and thanks to Allah ﷻ for giving us the tawfiq to translate this book. He has guided us and without Him, we would not have been guided to the straight path embodied by the Prophet Muḥammad ﷺ and the Ahl al-Bayt ﷺ.

This book is dedicated firstly to Ayatullāh Sayyid Ali Khamenei, who made tremendous strides in advancing the cause of Islam. It is also dedicated to all the scholars, martyrs and believers who worked tirelessly to promote the pure Muḥammadan path.

We want to also give our thanks and appreciation to all believers from around the world and acknowledge the team which helped al-Burāq Publications complete this work, spending countless hours to make its publication possible. Please recite Sūrah al-Fātiḥah on behalf of them and their marhūmēn.

This book is dedicated in honor of the following individuals. Please remember them in your prayers and may Allah ﷻ have mercy on them and their loved ones.

Abdul-Ameer Mohammad Ali Alkhafaji

Ahmad Chit	Hajji Halime Assi
Ali Ahmed Ftouni	Hajji Iman Elsaghir
Ali Aoun	Hajji Imane Srour
Alya Victoria Agemy Yazback	Hajji Mariam Omais
Band e Khuda	Hajji Miri Srour
Basheerunnisa Begum	Hajji Noura Bicher
Begum D. Amir	Hajji Sabah Kanso
Haji Nawal Daoud Nagdie	Hajji Zeinab Sharif Ismail
Hajj Abed Said Hammoud	Hemayath Ali Naqvi
Hajj Ahmad Ali Daoud	Humayun Ali Baig
Hajj Ali Chami	Izzat Aoun
Hajj Ali Hammoud	Khadije Aoun
Hajj Ali Youssef Amin Dabaja	Khursheed Begum
Hajj Amin Fahs	Mohammad Hossein Houshyar
Hajj Haidar Alaouie	Mohammed Husain Jafri
Hajj Hassan Mahmoud Sobh	Nadira Sultana
Hajj Ibrahim Fouani	Ramzeah Naji
Hajj Mohammad Ali Mahmoud	Sabiha Jafri
Hajj Moslem Srour	Sayed Mustapha Shukr
Hajj Mostafa Fouani	Shahid Kassem Ali Elkhatib
Hajj Sami Ali Ftouni	Shahla Sadeghipour
Hajj Yahya Kanso	Syed Irtiza Husain Rizvi
Hajj Yehya Fouani	Syed Mohammad Amir

Hajji Adiba Hadous

Hajji Amneh Mahmoud Sobh-Ftouni

Hajji Fatima Ankouni

Hajji Fawzieh Shukr

Syed Mujtaba Husain Rizvi

Syed Nurul Hasan Jafri

Syeda Saeeda Begum

Turfah Kassem Sobh

Duaa al-Hujja

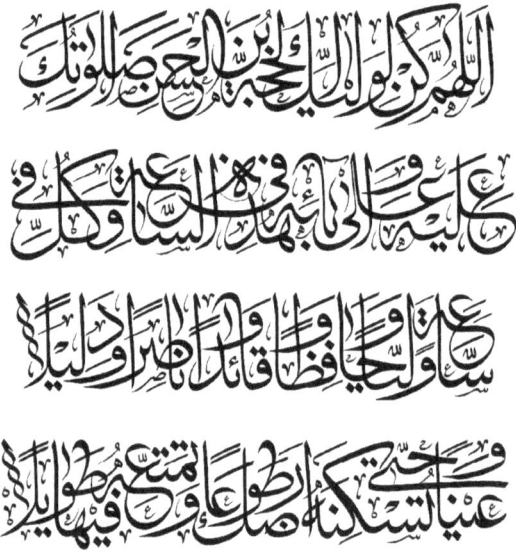

O Allah, be, for Your representative, the Hujjat (proof), son of al-Hasan, Your blessings be upon him and his forefathers, in this hour and in every hour: a guardian, a protector, a leader, a helper, a proof, and an eye - until You make him live on the Earth, in obedience (to You), and cause him to live in it for a long time.

Transliteration Table

The method of transliteration of Islamic terminology from the Arabic language has been carried out according to the standard transliteration table below.

ء	ʾ	ر	r	ف	f
ا	a	ز	z	ق	q
ب	b	س	s	ك	k
ت	t	ش	sh	ل	l
ث	th	ص	ṣ	م	m
ج	j	ض	ḍ	ن	n
ح	ḥ	ط	ṭ	و	w
خ	kh	ظ	ẓ	ه	h
د	d	ع	ʿ	ي	y
ذ	dh	غ	gh		

Long Vowels

ا	ā	و	ū	ي	ī

Short Vowels

◌َ	a	◌ُ	u	◌ِ	i

Table of Contents

About the Author 1

Preface 9

Marriage: The Law of Nature and the Constitution of the Sharia .. 15

    #1: Marriage is One of the Islamic Values 17

    #2: The Islamic Approach is the Best Approach 18

    #3: Establishing a Family is a Divine Duty 19

    #4: Allah 🌸 Does Not Favor Celibacy 19

    #5: The Prophet's 🌸 Sunnah: Marriage at the Right Timing .. 21

    #6: Early Marriage 22

    #7: The Facilitation of Marriage 24

    #8: Restrictions from the Age of Jahiliyyah 25

    #9: Make Things Easy and Allah 🌸 Will Suffice You .. 26

    #10: Wasteful Formalities 28

    #11: Expensive Lounges and Hotels 30

    #12: The Confusion of Some Officials 32

    #13: Big Halls Do Not Imply a Higher Degree of Honor 33

    #14: Facilitating Marriage 34

#15: Supporting Those in Need 35

#16: Follow the Household of the Prophet ﷺ 37

#17: The Wedding Garments 38

#18: The Dowry is a Symbol of Love 39

#19: Fourteen Gold Coins 41

#20: Expensive Dowries are Harmful 43

#21: Expensive Dowries are Not Guarantees 44

#22: Expensive Dowries are Harmful to Society 45

#23: The Bridal Trousseau (Jihāz) 47

#24: Bragging About Wedding Furniture 48

#25: Taking Others Into Consideration 50

#26: The Dowry of the Best Wife in the World ۞ 51

#27: Confronting the Traditions of Jahiliyyah 53

The Blessings and Benefits of Marriage 57

#28: Marriage is the Tranquility of the Soul 59

#29: Sharing Concerns is Truly Supportive 61

#30: Spouses are Adornments for One Another 61

#31: Home of Solace and Joy 62

#32: An Opportunity to Reclaim Vitality 65

#33: Establishing a Family 66

#34: Entering Paradise 69

#35: Being Grateful for the Gift of Marriage 74

#36: Practical Gratitude 76

The Importance of Succeeding in Creating a Family 81

#37: The Wellbeing of Society Arises from the Wellbeing of the Family 83

#38: The Absence of the Family is the Basis of Psychological Problems 84

#39: The Family is the Basis of Education 85

#40: The Family is the Spring of Culture 88

#41: The Family is a Person's Comfort 89

#42: The More Stable Family Benefits the Most 91

#43: The Role of Women and Men in a Family 92

#44: Love in Islamic Families 93

On Choosing a Spouse 97

#45: Excessive Idealism 99

#46: Competence from the Islamic Viewpoint 99

The Secret to a Happy Marriage 107

#47: Religiosity is the Secret to Family Survival 109

#48: Love is the Fundamental Issue 110

#49: The Greater the Love, the Better 111

#50: Taking Care of One Another 112

#51: Love is Not an Order 114

#52: Love and Self-Love 115

#53: Mutual Respect 116

#54: Degrading the Wife is the Beginning of the Family's Destruction 117

#55: Building Trust 118

#56: Love's Requirements 120

#57: Trust is Not a Contractual Agreement 120

#58: Mutual Understanding and Consideration 121

#59: Sexual Chastity 122

#60: Chastity and the Ḥijāb: The Stronghold of the Family ..123

#61: The Philosophy of the Ḥijab and Chastity....................... 126

#62: Enjoin one Another to the Truth and Patience 128

#63: Moral Supervision is a Form of Care................................ 129

#64: Triggering Jealousy and Envy... 129

#65: Safeguarding Marital Secrets 130

#66: Mutual Harmony 130

#67: Imām Khomeini: "Go and Get Along" 131

#68: What does Harmony Mean? 132

#69: Understanding the Other Person 134

#70: Refraining from Negative Intervention 135

The Western Predicament 139

#71: The Western Family.. 141

#72: The West's Biggest Sin 143

#73: Women's Loneliness... 144

#74: Sexual Freedom and the Collapse of the Family 144

#75: Moral Decay is the Cause of the Collapse........................ 145

#76: Artificial Love.. 146

#77: Artificial Families 147

#78: The Age of Marriage 147

#79: The Collapse of Family Due to Inappropriate Age 148

#80: The Family Conditions in the West 150

#81: Will Anyone Listen? 151

#82: The Family and Identity 152

#83: A Speech on Family 154

Mutual Rights of the Husband and Wife 157

#84: Modern Society's Oppression of Women 163

#85: Man's Oppression of Women 165

#86: Mutual Rights 165

#87: A Woman is a Sweet Basil 169

#88: A Woman is a Flower, Not a Business Manager 171

#89: A Man is a Trustee and a Woman is a Sweet Basil 172

#90: Exchanging Roles is Prohibited 173

#91: The Man Must Work 174

#92: Partnership Not Mastery 175

#93: The Natural Difference Between Men and Women 175

#94: Taking the Woman's Opinion into Consideration 177

Work Division 183

#95: Work Division 185

#96: Providing Moral Support 187

#97: Women's Work 189

#98: The Finest Types of Support 189

#99: The Importance of House Work 191

#100: Childcare is a Great Skill 192

#101: Work-Life Balance 193

About the Author

Imām Sayyid Ali Khamenei is among Shi'a Islam's leading religious authorities and is the second Supreme Leader of the Islamic Republic of Iran. Before being elected as the Leader in 1989, he was president for two terms and a member of parliament for a short period. The late Imām Khomeini also chose him to lead the Friday Prayer in Tehran.

His Family

On the 16th of July 1939, the future Leader of Islamic Republic was born in the holy city of Mashhad, in the province of Khorasan in Iran. Sayyid Ali was the second son of Sayyid Jawad Khamenei (d. 1986), a humble and well-known Islamic scholar, and Khadija Mirdamadi (d. 1989) a pious and devout follower of the religion.

Education

Under the supervision of his father, Sayyid Ali started his seminary education at the age of 9.

In 1957, he attended the advanced level of seminary education (Kharij) under Ayatullāh Sayyid Muhammad Hadi Milani. He made a short trip to Najaf with his family and participated in the seminaries of famous teachers. However, due to his father's disinclination for staying in Najaf, Sayyid Ali returned to Mashhad and attended for one more year in the class of Ayatullāh Milani and then moved to the seminaries of Qom to study under some of the leading scholars of the time from 1958 to 1964.

Ayatullāh Khamenei would then return to Mashhad to help his father who suffered eyesight problems and attended again in the sessions of Ayatullāh Milani until 1970.

Teaching

Since the time he was in Mashhad, he taught jurisprudence and principles of jurisprudence (including the books Rasa'il, Makasib, and Kifaya) and held public sessions of commentary of the Qur'an. From 1969 onwards, he began teaching a unique course of commentary of the Qur'an for Islamic students, which continued until 1977 before being exiled to Iranshahr. After he had become the Supreme Leader of Iran, he began teaching advanced level seminaries classes (kharij), and this has been continuing until today.

Teachers

Ayatullāh Khamenei has been a student of many established scholars, some of which include:

- Sayyid Jalil Husayni Sistani

- Ayatullāh Sayyid Jawad Khamenei

- Mirza Muhammad Mudarris Yazdi

- Ayatullāh Sayyid Muhammad Hadi Milani

- Ayatullāh Burujirdi

- Imām Khomeini

- Ayatullāh Shaykh Murtada Ha'iri Yazdi

- Ayatullāh Sayyid Muhammad Muhaqqiq Damad

- Allamah Tabataba'i

Literature

Ayatullāh Khamenei is well versed with poetry and literature and has always been interested in reading novels, in addition to the history and culture of different nations. He remains in contact with many poets, writers and intellectuals, sharing much interest with them in an array of different literature works.

Ayatullāh Khamenei himself has composed some poems, and he has used the pen name "Amin" ["trustworthy"] in recent years.

Political Activities

It was in Qum, in 1962, that Ayatullāh Khamenei joined the ranks of the revolutionary followers of Imām Khomeini who opposed the pro-Western, anti-Islamic policies of the Shah. Despite persecution, torture, imprisonment and exile, Ayatullāh Khamenei remained dedicated and fearless; he followed this path for the next 16 years, which ultimately led to the downfall of the Shah's brutal regime.

From May 1963 onwards, Ayatullāh Khamenei was known for his Islamic activism and lessons on the

commentary of the Holy Qur'an, the Prophetic Traditions and Islamic ideology in Mashhad and Tehran. Watched closely by Shah's intelligence agency, the SAVAK, he was forced to go underground in 1967.

Being Appointed the Supreme Leader

After the demise of Imām Khomeini on June 4, 1989, the Assembly of Experts for Leadership held a session in the afternoon of the same day in which some members of the Assembly mentioned Imām Khomeini's opinion about the competence of Ayatullāh Khamenei for the leadership of the country. Then, there was an election, and the unanimous vote of the members of the Assembly chose Ayatullāh Khamenei as the new Supreme Leader of the Islamic Republic of Iran.

His Religious Authority

In 1994, the Assembly of Teachers of the seminary of Qom and the Community of Combatant Clerics of Tehran announced that they see Ayatullāh Khamenei as a competent jurist for being followed by the masses. However, in a speech, Ayatullāh Khamenei emphasized that there is no need for the masses to follow him jurisprudentially in Iran since there were many qualified jurists already fulfilling this duty. Today, millions around the world follow his jurisprudential opinions.

Preface

*In the Name of Allāh, the Most Gracious,
the Most Merciful*

﴿وَمِنْ آيَاتِهِ أَنْ خَلَقَ لَكُم مِّنْ أَنفُسِكُمْ أَزْوَاجًا لِّتَسْكُنُوا إِلَيْهَا وَجَعَلَ بَيْنَكُم مَّوَدَّةً وَرَحْمَةً إِنَّ فِي ذَٰلِكَ لَآيَاتٍ لِّقَوْمٍ يَتَفَكَّرُونَ﴾

﴿And of His signs is that He created for you mates from your own selves that you may take comfort in them, and He ordained affection and mercy between you﴾

Perhaps we read this blessed verse many times, or it echoed in our ears at every wedding; and perhaps we thought about its meaning and interpretation as well. However, the word of Allah is an inexhaustible sea, and its bottom is of unfathomable depth; and everyone who enters it comes out of it anew. And if, in this verse, we shed light on the words "affection and mercy," we realize that the foundation of the family – as Allah wants it to be – must be based on these two great pillars. Any family that loses the pillar of affection or that of mercy runs the risk of being destroyed and ceases to be a family; it rather transforms into a materialistic relationship between the two spouses or a relationship in which one spouse dominates and controls the other. Meanwhile, we notice that within the affectionate family, the spouse sacrifices his most precious possessions for the sake of his partner, not for anything material and without expecting of him any compensation or reward, but solely because he loves him.

This affection may even develop throughout their relationship, with time, in such a way that the relationship itself becomes that of mercy and companionship, in contrary to what some people think when they claim that marriage is "love's graveyard". No, the marriage that is founded on affection and mercy can never be a graveyard for love; rather, in such a marriage, the spouse becomes unable to live without his partner for even a few moments.

Circumstances may also lead to one of the spouses becoming chronically ill or disabled. In a marriage founded on mercy, the spouse does not abandon his afflicted partner regardless of the price he has to pay, for, he deals with his spouse on the basis of mercy; and mercy is much finer, greater and broader than the concept of love.

That's how Islam built the marital relationship; and that is how it established the family. For the sake of ensuring that our beloved families in our communities delight in warmth, affection, and happiness we have chosen the most important pieces of advice that were provided by the Guardian of the Muslims, Sayyid Ali Khamenei, to married couples before concluding their marital contract, so they can build their lives on the basis of real-life awareness and mindfulness of this new establishment and promising family.

We hope that this piece of work contributes to the aim we pursue, which is the happiness of married couples in every home; and we hope, with this effort, to gain the pleasure of the Imām of our time ﷻ.

Chapter One

Marriage: The Law of Nature and the Constitution of the Sharia

Marriage: The Law of Nature and the Constitution of the Sharia

#1: Marriage is One of the Islamic Values

The Islamic viewpoint which stems from the book of Allah and the Sunnah of his Prophet is clear in its implications; as it encourages and promotes marriage – nay it gives marriage a rare status, whereby the blessed Prophet says, "There is no establishment in Islam that is more beloved to Allah than marriage."[1]

And this is what the Guardian of the Muslims, Sayyid Ali Khamenei, refers to:

"The primary and fundamental issue is that marriage which Allah made a Sunnah - and which human nature also requires - is one of the divine secrets and blessings, and one of the inevitable phenomena in human life. For Allah could have let people make their own decisions when it came to marriage without ruling the latter as mandatory or permissible; however, He considered marriage to be one of the values, and that he who did not marry had wasted that value."[2]

---

[1] *Wasā'il al-Shī'a*, part 14, page 3

[2] The Contract Speech dated 6/10/1372 S.H.

#2: The Islamic Approach is the Best Approach

"Christianity, Judaism and other religions also have the likes of these guidelines for marriage, but in a different way; and Islam has accepted these guidelines and considered them (the spouses) husband and wife and their children legitimate."[3]

"The manner in which marriage takes place under Islam is better that that under other religions and amongst other people, whether in regard to its premises, foundation, or continuity. All marriages were legislated to the advantage of the human being. Marriages in other religions are respected and recognized by us. That is to say that the contracts that are concluded in churches or synagogues or by any other people - in whichever way possible - are recognized by us; and we do not consider them invalid with respect to their parties. However, the approach defined by Islam is better because Islam emphasized the fact that there are rights for the man, rights for the woman, manners within the marital relationship, and a special approach to

---

[3] The Contract Speech dated 11/5/1375 S.H.

marriage. And the basis to all this is the preservation of the family unit and the happiness of the family."[4]

#3: Establishing a Family is a Divine Duty

"According to Islam, establishing a family is considered a divine duty; and it is an action that must be carried out by the man and the woman as a divine obligation. And even though establishing a family wasn't mentioned amongst the legislated Sharia obligations, it was highly encouraged in such a way that it is understood that Allah emphasizes this matter not as a legislation, but rather as a perpetual and influential occurrence in life and society. That's the reason behind all this encouragement to maintain the bond between the husband and wife, and behind the disapproval of their separation."[5]

#4: Allah Does Not Favor Celibacy

"The young man who is able to get married but doesn't, and the young woman who wants to get married and refuses the suitors - under the pretext that the time has not come yet, are not – in my opinion – honest in their feelings and words. Let

---

[4] The Contract Speech dated 19/1/1377 S.H.

[5] The Contract Speech dated 11/12/1377 S.H.

them consult their sexual instincts, so that the answer can come from those glands that secrete [hormones] into the blood, rather than the tongue. They may also try to address the question to their blessed Prophet Muḥammad b. ʿAbdillāh, so he may answer them openly:

"Marriage is my Sunnah; and whoever does not follow my Sunnah is not from me."[6]

And Sayyid Khamenei says:

"Allah does not favor the single man and the single woman, especially the youth who haven't gotten married until now – and this is not restricted to the youth. Allah loves the shared life.[7] It is undesirable, from the Islamic viewpoint, for a person to spend his life alone; as he would be an alien in the midst of the human structure. Islam wanted the family – and not the single individual - to be the actual cellular unit in the overall social structure.[8]

---

[6] *Biḥār al-Anwār*, part 103, page 220

[7] The Contract Speech dated 20/11/1375 S.H.

[8] The Contract Speech dated 5/10/1375 S.H.

#5: The Prophet's ﷺ Sunnah: Marriage at the Right Timing

And his Eminence says:

"We have a well-known narration. It's that the Prophet ﷺ had said, 'Marriage is my Sunnah'; and it is surely the law of creation and that of all people, citizens and religions. Why, then, did the Prophet ﷺ say 'my Sunnah'? What is the secret behind this specification? Maybe the reason lies in the great emphasis on marriage under Islam which was lacking in other divine religions.

You notice that Islam's emphasis on marriage is unparalleled in the social schools, widespread philosophies, and prevalent policies in the world. Islam insists that the youth are to get married when they are ready for marriage."[9]

"Marriage, in addition to being a natural need, is a religious and Islamic Sunnah. Accordingly, it becomes very easy to get rewarded for an act that is required by necessity and the nature of creation."[10]

---

[9] The Contract Speech dated 28/6/1379 S.H.

[10] The Contract Speech dated 9/11/1376 S.H.

"Marriage is a divine and creational Sunnah; and when the blessed Prophet ﷺ mentions that marriage is his Sunnah, this means that Islam has given great emphasis to this issue. As for why? Well, this goes back to the importance of the subject matter and to the great influence of the family on the upbringing of the human being and his ethical perfection, and on building up the wholesome human being emotionally, spiritually and otherwise."[11]

#6: Early Marriage

And if marriage was desired instinctually, innately and Islamically then the Muslim man or woman must take the initiative towards marriage in their youth, so they may stave off the pressure of desire and block one of the devil's biggest doors.

And his Eminence says:

"The Prophet ﷺ used to emphasize early marriage among the youth – be it young men or women, which would certainly be carried out by their own desire and choice rather than someone else's. We should definitely work on promoting this within our communities. The youth must marry at an

---

[11] The Contract Speech dated 29/4/1379 S.H.

appropriate age before leaving the period of their youth, the age of vitality and desire. This is in contrary to the understanding of many who believe that marriage while young is immature and unstable. In fact, the opposite is true; and things are not as they claim. For, if a marriage was carried out properly, then it would be stable and sound; and the relationship between the man and the woman would be very intimate in such a household."[12]

His Eminence says:

"Islam insists that marriage should be carried out at the right time, that is, once the need for it arises; and this is one of Islam's features. The faster the marriage is carried out, the better. And by 'faster' we mean the time at which the offspring in a family, whether male or female, feel the need for marriage, in which case the faster this need is met, the better. And the reason behind this is as follows:

First, marriage has certain blessings and bounties which befall the person who gets married in due time, that is, before time passes him by.

---
[12] The Contract Speech dated 23/12/1379 S.H.

Secondly, it prevents the revolution of the sexual instinct; that's why it is said that 'he who gets married has fulfilled half his religion.' This narration implies that half the risks which inflict a person's religion rise from the revolution of the sexual instinct; and this is a very large number."[13]

#7: The Facilitation of Marriage

And since Islam favors early marriage, then the Islamic community must strive to facilitate the marriage of young men and women.

His Eminence says:

"If you observe the marriage ceremonies among different peoples, you will find that the marriage ceremony in Islam is quite easy and simple. Celebrations, enjoyments and the likes of which are certainly permissible – for each has his own taste; however, they are not part of the religious formalities and etiquettes of marriage.

Anyone has the right to hold these celebrations or forsake them as they wish. As for the obligation of going to a temple and bowing in front of someone,

---

[13] The Contract Speech dated 9/12/1380 S.H.

and doing what they do, or the ceremonies that exist in other places, these are all nonexistent in Islam. The only ritual that exists in Islam is a religious formula that must be recited."[14]

#8: Restrictions from the Age of Jahiliyyah[15]

"The sacred Islamic Sharia eliminated the restrictions that were present in Jahiliyyah and the conditions that were customary among ignorant people in regards to marriage, and legislated a series of new things, conditions and laws. If we behave in a way that our marriages and marital contracts are free from things that Islam has eradicated, adorning them with the laws established by Islam, then our contract and marriage will be Islamic and in accordance with what satisfies the Prophet of Islam and great leader of mankind ﷺ. And in case we include within the marriage contract – Allah forbid – that which Islam has eradicated and tossed away, then our contract will be that of Jahiliyyah. We will be Muslims but our behavior will belong to Jahiliyyah. And if we do not take into consideration

---

[14] The Contract Speech dated 28/6/1379 S.H.

[15] Translator's note: the era which preceded Islam, often referred to as the Age of Ignorance or al-*Jahiliyyah*.

the matters established by Islam in regards to marriage, then our contract will not be fully Islamic as well.

And if the contract is Islamic and in line with the Qurʾānic laws established by Islam, then life will be beautiful and the married couple will live a pleasant life."[16]

#9: Make Things Easy and Allah ﷻ Will Suffice You

"When we have a conversation with the youth, they say, 'If we get married, what will we do afterwards?' These are the restrictions that always hinder the fundamental and significant affairs.

Allah ﷻ says,

⟨*If they are poor, Allah will enrich them out of His grace*⟩[17]

This means that Allah ﷻ will make sure to suffice them if they get married. Marriage does not create specific difficulties in your living conditions; on the

---

[16] The Contract Speech dated 22/1/1374 S.H.

[17] Sūrat al-Nūr, Verse 32.

contrary, Allah ﷻ will enrich you from His grace, as He ﷻ says Himself. Yes, as the saying goes, we work wastefully rather than prudently; and we create illusionary needs and additional concerns. Certainly, then, problems will arise; and whose fault is it? It's the fault of the rich, first and foremost.

Those who are financially capable raise the bar of ambitions, inclinations, and false necessities to its peak. Some official people in charge are also at fault; as they should be raising these issues and providing means but they aren't. I don't intend to say that the government doesn't have a role in regards to the youth and their marriages; however, it needs to be clarified within the Islamic community that marriage is necessary and must be carried out and implemented.

What is being said by young women in regards to not being ready for marriage, or by young men in regards to not having the sufficient intellectual maturity is largely illogical; as we realize that in other aspects of life, this isn't the case. Young people are quite excellent and have the sufficient competence and understanding. However, marriage means bearing responsibility; therefore, the tendency to evade this responsibility is what keeps them from taking this initiative."[18]

#10: Wasteful Formalities

"Formalities are harmful to society; and those who oppose formalities are not ignorant of their pleasure and delight. No! They rather consider them harmful to society like a harmful medicine or drink, for society is harmed because of these excessive formalities. Yes, they are acceptable if done within the bounds of reason and custom; however, once they become a matter of competition, they exceed their limits and diverge into other directions."[19]

"Some people are wasteful and spendthrift. And in this age when there are poor people in society who are denied the fundamentals of life, these actions are considered wasteful, improvident and irresponsible. And everyone who acts in such a way is considered to have committed a wrongful act.[20]

"Some people commit sins through an action through which they can gain reward, all because of

---

[18] The Contract Speech dated 28/6/1379 S.H.

[19] The Contract Speech dated 20/4/1370 S.H.

[20] The Contract Speech dated 11/6/1372 S.H.

their wasteful behavior, prohibited deeds, and mixing up this good deed with prohibited ones. The prohibition is not restricted to a mixed gathering between a foreign man and woman and so on. This is certainly prohibited. Nonetheless, overspending and wastefulness are prohibited as well. Breaking the hearts of poor people in some situations is certainly prohibited. Excessiveness and making things permissible or prohibited based on whims so that a father can prepare the wedding furniture for his daughter are all prohibited acts."[21]

"I am not pleased with those complicate the process of marriage for others due to costly and wasteful expenses. We certainly approve of celebration and enjoyment; however we object to overspending.[22] How many men and women – who even if they get married – feel inferior and tormented due to the carelessness of the rich? They would even develop a complexity by which they would feel impoverished and then start to blame themselves for it."[23]

---

[21] The Contract Speech dated 9/11/1376 S.H.

[22] The Contract Speech dated 24/5/1374 S.H.

[23] The Contract Speech dated 5/10/1375 S.H.

#11: Expensive Lounges and Hotels

"Leave these expensive hotels, halls and celebrations. It's certainly permissible to have a modest celebration in a wedding hall. I don't want to generalize since some people do not have the means or their homes are not big enough. However, avoid overspending. Joyfulness, celebration and inviting friends and relatives are a good thing; however, overspending is wrong and inappropriate for our Muslim people."[24]

"And the contract, marriage and wedding are all good things; even the blessed Prophet ﷺ celebrated the marriage of his blessed daughter ﷺ, where people recited poetry and women clapped and rejoiced. However, there shouldn't be wastefulness in marriage gatherings. This wastefulness is manifested in expensive marriage ceremonies that take place in luxurious and overpriced halls and hotels where plenty of money is spent on desserts, fruits, and food that eventually get spoiled or thrown to the ground. And for what? For the sake of competition, so that they do not fall behind in the caravan of extravagance."[25]

---

[24] The Contract Speech dated 27/10/1373 S.H.

[25] The Contract Speech dated 15/1/1372 S.H.

"There shouldn't be any wastefulness; and if there is, then you have inflicted harm upon yourselves and upon young men and women. You have also cast yourselves from the eye of the Prophet of Islam and the eyes of the Imām of our time, for wastefulness and excessiveness are considered prohibited acts."[26]

"A happy marriage is not that which involves a lot of spending and extravagance. A happy marriage is the intimate marriage. If a marriage is intimate it becomes happy even if it is simple. When friends and relatives gather in one or two rooms of the house, then it is considered a marriage ceremony. As for the extravagant ceremonies, expensive halls and hotels, high expenses and overpriced products needed for such ceremonies, this is all inappropriate. I am not saying that it annuls the marriage, no; the marriage remains valid. However, it disrupts the atmosphere within the community."[27]

"These halls and such things did not exist in the past. They used to celebrate in a room or two, and the guests would come and have some desserts.

---

[26] The Contract Speech dated 1/11/1371 S.H.

[27] The Contract Speech dated 12/9/1377 S.H.

Were those marriages less blessed than the marriages of today?

And were the girls back then less esteemed than today, such that they now need to go to these big halls? It's fine, I do not reject these halls; however I reject the exaggerated ceremonies. For instance, going to hotels is one of the unnecessary wrongful acts."[28]

"The simpler and shorter the ceremony is, the better. Let those with limited means be encouraged to get married and do not allow them to fall into despair."[29]

#12: The Confusion of Some Officials

"It is currently well-known that there are celebrations that take place in hotels and other things that happen in clubs. This is first and foremost inappropriate for people of knowledge, the faithful and the pious. This was the path of people in the past. Unfortunately, some people today misunderstand things and claim that since former officials and rulers behaved in a certain way then

---

[28] The Contract Speech dated 30/7/1376 S.H.

[29] The Contract Speech dated 24/9/1371 S.H.

they – after becoming rulers themselves - should follow the same path!

No, those were tyrants – they were worldly people. Meanwhile we are religious scholars, and those who are not religious scholars are still religious. Our lives are different, our behavior is different, our nature is different, our ethics are different, and our goals are fundamentally different from theirs. We must not imitate them; rather, we must behave in such a way that is appropriate for us so that people imitate us."[30]

#13: Big Halls Do Not Imply a Higher Degree of Honor

"Some people assume that formalities, going to certain hotels, expensive halls and steep expenses increase the honor of the son or daughter. No! The son or daughter's honor lies in piety, chastity and knowledge, not in those things."[31]

"Know that simplicity in marriage, whether in regards to the dowry, the wedding furniture, or the marriage ceremony, is not a shame. Some people assume that if we arrange a simple marriage

---

[30] The Contract Speech dated 11/5/1374 S.H.

[31] The Contract Speech dated 11/5/1375 S.H.

ceremony for our daughter then she will be humiliated. No, she won't! You are mistaken."[32]

#14: Facilitating Marriage

"My advice to all people across the country is to facilitate marriage. Some people complicate marriage. Expensive dowries and furniture render marriage problematic. Why do families request expensive furniture? And why do girls' families exaggerate with the wedding furniture and marriage ceremony? Is it so that they could compete with others? Why? Do they know the impact of this behavior? Its impact is that young men remain unmarried and do not dare to think of marriage."[33]

"Are the ones who have a pretentious marriage ceremony happier than those who have a simple ceremony? Who can make such an estimation? These actions cause nothing more than sowing pain in the hearts of young men and women and making their lives bitter if they couldn't get married in the same way others did. Therefore, either this pain remains in their hearts forever or they never manage to get married. Once a suitor proposes to marry

---

[32] The Contract Speech dated 18/9/1375 S.H.

[33] The Contract Speech dated 2/9/1373 S.H.

someone's daughter, this girl will stay at home because the suitor doesn't own anything, and this university student or worker or poor employee will remain unmarried."[34]

"I think those who make things more difficult, in terms of huge gatherings, celebrations and expensive dowries and furniture, will have a very tough reckoning with Allah. They cannot say, 'We have money and we want to do whatever we wish for, because we own this money.' These words are wrong. The fact that we have money is not an excuse. If someone has money, does it allow him to behave in such a way that leaves others unable to act and young men hesitant about getting married? It is not permissible to behave in a way that deters people who lack the financial means, or those who do not want to get married or are not convinced of it, or those who have different intentions."[35]

#15: Supporting Those in Need

"Be neither wasteful nor extravagant. Do not commit such actions, for, they are disadvantageous, and the divine legislator also disapproves of them. Know

---

[34] The Contract Speech dated 23/9/1373 S.H.

[35] The Contract Speech dated 24/5/1374 S.H.

also that you will be creating unnecessary hardships for yourselves. Rather than making all these expenses, give tenth of them to someone in need and gain the reward."[36]

"If you want to conclude your marital contract in a certain hotel, overspend on the ceremony, and offer new seasonal fruits, does your marriage gain luster and beauty?

It will certainly lack any divine reward. Know that this behavior does not gain any reward from Allah; that is, if overspending was not a sin – and it is – then it would definitely lack any gain or reward.

However, by these actions, you will deprive hundreds of young men and women from celebrating their wedding. They will observe and try to catch up with you yet fail to do so; and that's why their marriage gets delayed."[37]

---

[36] The Contract Speech dated 19/2/1374 S.H.
[37] The Contract Speech dated 22/8/1376 S.H.

#16: Follow the Household of the Prophet ﷺ

"The best woman in the world is Lady Fāṭima al-Zahrāʾ Fāṭima al-Zahrāʾ ع, and the best man and husband in the world is the Commander of the Faithful ع. Observe them; how did they get married?

Thousands of handsome, wealthy, and fancied young men who come from esteemed families, do not amount to a single hair on the head of the Commander of the Faithful Imām ʿAlī b. Abī Ṭālib ع. And thousands of beautiful girls who come from esteemed households do not amount to a single hair on the head of Fāṭima al-Zahrāʾ Fāṭima al-Zahrāʾ ع. These two were of high standing with Allah and among the greats of their time. Fāṭima ع was the daughter of the Prophet ﷺ, the leader of the Islamic nation and its absolute ruler, and ʿAlī ع was the first person who waged jihād in Islam. Observe how they got married – how little was the dowry and how simple the wedding furniture; everything was in the name and remembrance of Allah. These are our role models.

At that time, there were ignorant people as well who would exaggerate their daughters' dowries and raise them to a thousand she-camels, for instance.

Were they better than the Prophet's daughter? Therefore, do not imitate those people and follow the Prophet's daughter. Follow the Commander of the Faithful.[38]

#17: The Wedding Garments

"Some people purchase expensive garments for the wedding night. This isn't necessary. If they need a wedding suit, they can rent one. What's the problem with that? Is it a disgrace? No. What's disgraceful about that? And what's problematic about it? Some people may find it disgraceful, yet the disgrace lies in wasting one's money by purchasing something that will only be used once and then thrown away. Using something only once, and under these conditions suffered by some people! Some are really in need."[39]

---

[38] The Contract Speech dated 17/2/1375 S.H.

[39] The Contract Speech dated 4/10/1374 S.H.

#18: The Dowry is a Symbol of Love

"The blessed Prophet ﷺ destroyed the tradition of Jahiliyyah in regards to the dowry. The person who legislated the dowry – i.e. the Prophet ﷺ – is the best of all creatures, His pure and esteemed daughter is the best of women of all worlds – from the first and the last; and her husband is the Commander of the Faithful who is the best man after the Prophet ﷺ among all mankind. Did you observe the dowry stipulated by the Prophet ﷺ for these two people ﷺ, who were young, beautiful, esteemed and of the best in Medina?"[40]

"The Prophet ﷺ destroyed those things since they prevented young men and women from getting married; he requested that these things be abandoned.

The beginning of marriage is easy; and it is easier from the financial aspect. The important thing in marriage is to take being humane into consideration."[41]

---

[40] The Contract Speech dated 24/9/1371 S.H.

[41] The Contract Speech dated 6/10/1372 S.H.

"Don't think that expensive dowries and huge pieces of furniture were inaccessible at that time. No, they had mindless people back then, as we do now, who used to demand that their daughters' dowries be equivalent to a million measurements (mithqāl) of gold, for instance - the exact parallel to the foolishness committed by some people nowadays. These exaggerated trends initially belonged to ignorant people; then Islam came and abolished them entirely. Was the Prophet incapable of demanding that the dowry of his daughter be equivalent to a thousand red camels of specific qualifications? He was able to do that. However, Islam came and eliminated all these matters."[42]

"The expensive dowry is of the traditions of Jahiliyyah; and the blessed Prophet abolished it.

The Prophet was from a family of notables. The Prophet's family was almost the biggest family of the notables of Quraysh; and he himself was the community leader. So what was problematic about demanding an expensive dowry for his daughter, who reached this level of perfection that made her the best woman of all worlds from the first to the

---

[42] The Contract Speech dated 12/11/1372 S.H.

last – and Allah considered her as such – and who wanted to get married to the best man in the world – the Master of the Pious? Why did the Prophet reduce this dowry which is called the Dowry of the Sunnah (mahr al-sunna)?[43]"[44]

"I think that such simplicity in regards to Lady Fāṭima's wedding furniture and dowry, and the strict adoption and preservation of this small dowry (Dowry of the Sunnah) by all the household of the Prophet at times when everyone knew that it was permissible to surpass it had a symbolic value; it became a basis according to which people would interact in order to avoid the problems that arise out of overspending."[45]

#19: Fourteen Gold Coins

"We mentioned that a marital contract is limited to a dowry of fourteen gold coins. This does not mean that the amount which exceeds this limit jeopardizes the validity of the marriage, no! Even if the dowry was equivalent to fourteen thousand gold coins, the marriage would still be valid; it doesn't make any

---

[43] *Al-Kāfī*, part 5, chapter *al-Sunna Fī al-Muhūr*, page 375, Ḥadīth 7.

[44] The Contract Speech dated 28/2/11374 S.H.

[45] The Contract Speech dated 18/4/1377 S.H.

difference in this regard. Rather, this is so that the moral aspect in marriage outweighs its material aspect such that it does not become a sort of trade or material transaction. If you reduce the formalities, then the moral aspect will become stronger."[46]

"And the lesser the dowry is, the closer it gets to the nature of marriage, for the nature of marriage does not resemble a transaction, a sale, a purchase, or a rent; rather, it is the life of two persons. This is not related to material things. The sacred Legislator decided to establish a dowry, but it must not be expensive. It must, rather, be normal and accessible to everyone."[47]

"Marriage entails a humane phenomenon and connection, not a financial or material transaction, even though a monetary value is prescribed by the sacred Legislator. This money has a symbolic and representative quality; and it is not a sale, purchase, or a trade."[48]

---

[46] The Contract Speech dated 26/10/1372 S.H.

[47] The Contract Speech dated 18/5/1374 S.H.

[48] The Contract Speech dated 5/1/1371 S.H.

#20: Expensive Dowries are Harmful

"If someone cares for his daughter, or if there is a girl who respects herself, then the appropriate way to express this is not by demanding an expensive dowry. The lesser the dowry is, the more humane this relationship will be."[49]

"There is no amount of money or wealth that is equivalent to the value of a human being. And there isn't any dowry that can be equivalent to the fingertip of a Muslim woman. And there isn't any income that can be equivalent to a Muslim man's character. Those who raise their daughters' dowries as a sign of respect for them are mistaken; this is not respectful, it is harmful. When you raise the value of the dowry, you reduce the value of this humane transaction and place one of its parties at the same level of a commodity or a product, whereby they say, 'my daughter is worth this much.'

"Your daughter must never be valued in terms of money. This dowry is a divine and Islamic Sunnah; it is not intended to be offered in exchange for this honorable and precious human being."[50]

---

[49] The Contract Speech dated 24/5/1374 S.H.

[50] The Contract Speech dated 11/8/1377 S.H.

#21: Expensive Dowries are Not Guarantees

"Sometimes the man is in a position which causes the woman – regardless of her expensive dowry – to say, 'I'll give up my dowry to save myself.' A dowry doesn't make anyone happy. It is but the religious path that makes people happy. And love is not associated with these things; in fact, the less the amount of money is and the further away the material aspect, the stronger the humane aspect becomes and the greater the love will be."[51]

"Some people assume that expensive dowries contribute to preserving the marital bond; this is incorrect and misleading. If the married couple – Allah forbid – are incompatible, then the expensive dowry will not create a miracle."[52]

"The girl's parents may say, 'We do not want an expensive dowry.' However, the groom's family – for the sake of boasting and bragging – might say, "No! The dowry can never be less than millions.' All this is far from Islam; an expensive dowry does not bring anyone happiness. These people believe that if the

---

[51] The Contract Speech dated 10/2/1375 S.H.

[52] The Contract Speech dated 11/5/1375 S.H.

dowry is inexpensive then the marriage will break down. These people are mistaken. If the marriage is built on love, and in a proper manner, then it will never break, even in the absence of a dowry. However, if it is built on malice, deceit, fraud, trickery and its likes, then – no matter how expensive the dowry is – the conceited and wicked man will behave in a way that will eventually relieve him from the burden of this dowry."[53]

"Some people say, 'We increase the dowry in order to prevent divorce.' This is very big mistake. Never has there been a dowry expensive enough that prevented or could prevent divorce. Divorce can only be prevented by ethics, behavior, and respecting the Islamic regulations."[54]

#22: Expensive Dowries are Harmful to Society

"Those who demand an expensive dowry for their women cause harm to society; many girls remain in their homes and many young men remain single. This is because these trends will become a social norm, a Sunnah and a custom, rather than having

---

[53] The Contract Speech dated 4/9/1375 S.H.

[54] The Contract Speech dated 2/9/1373 S.H.

the dowry of the Prophet ﷺ as the Sunnah. And when the dowry of Jahiliyyah becomes the Sunnah, then the conditions will be of that age as well."[55]

"If the material dimension becomes the foundation on which a marriage is built, then this emotional, spiritual and humane interaction will turn into a materialistic one. Expensive furniture and boasting and bragging about money and wealth – which is done by heedless and ignorant people – in reality destroys the marriage. Accordingly, it is commendable (mustaḥabb) by the sacred Sharia that the dowry amount remains small and the Dowry of the Sunnah is taken into account."[56]

"And if dowries are expensive then marriage will encounter hardships; and young men and women will remain confused. Therefore, the more you facilitate things, the better."[57]

"I ask people from all across the country to refrain from increasing the dowry amounts to this extent, for this is the Sunnah of Jahiliyyah and an act with

---

[55] The Contract Speech dated 11/8/1377 S.H.

[56] The Contract Speech dated 13/12/1377 S.H.

[57] The Contract Speech dated 22/12/1372 S.H.

which Allah ﷻ and the Prophet ﷺ are not pleased, especially in this age. I am not saying that it is prohibited (ḥarām) and that the marriage is invalid. However, it goes against the Sunnah of the Prophet, his Household – the Imams of guidance– and the great people of Islam ﷺ; and it is incompatible with their tradition, especially in the present time when the country is in need of having its affairs carried out properly and easily. It isn't in the advantage of anyone to complicate marriage to this extent."[58]

#23: The Bridal Trousseau (*Jihāz*)

A woman's honor is in her morals rather than her trousseau:

"The bridal trousseau does not bestow honor upon the girl, for her honor is in her morals, behavior and personality. Some families exhaust and harm themselves. If they didn't have enough money, they would struggle to attain it, and if they had money, then they would spend it abundantly in pursuit of preparing extravagant and ornamented wedding furniture."[59]

---

[58] The Contract Speech dated 2/9/1373 S.H.

[59] The Contract Speech dated 28/12/1377 S.H.

"An expensive dowry and extravagant furniture do not bring happiness to any girl, nor do they bring stability, tranquility and the desired trust to any family. These things are on the margins of life and belong to its trivialities; they do not have any benefit nor do they provide anything but trouble, difficulties and problems. You shouldn't borrow money and put yourselves and families in trouble in order to prepare for the wedding furniture. You shouldn't think that it would be humiliating if your daughter's furniture was inferior to that of your neighbors' or relatives' daughter. No, this is not humiliating."[60]

#24: Bragging About Wedding Furniture

"Some families, out of ostentation, make a dilemma out of wedding furniture. And later, after enduring this dilemma, in one way or another, the turn in shouldering it moves to other people. When you prepare all these means as wedding furniture, how will it impact others who witness these means?

---

[60] The Contract Speech dated 29/3/1381 S.H.

Where will all this bragging lead eventually? These are the problems that will arise, and which Islam aims to avoid."[61]

"Some people compete, in preparing the wedding furniture, with all their relatives, neighbors, friends and acquaintances. And this is also improper. One must look for the right thing to do, and then do it. What is the righteous thing? It is that the family composed of two people has the sufficient means to live a simple life."[62]

"When they commit all sorts of wastefulness, overspending and wrongful acts, and when they buy expensive commodities and everything so they can include it in the bridal trousseau in order to have at least one extra item with which the girl gets to beat her cousin, sister, neighbor or colleague, this is a painful mistake that bothers the person concerned and others as well. A lot of girls cannot move to their marital home and a lot of young men cannot marry because of these issues and problems. If marriage was easy and people weren't as rigid, if some people's wedding furniture wasn't this

---

[61] The Contract Speech dated 16/3/1373 S.H.

[62] The Contract Speech dated 3/8/1379 S.H.

expensive, and had it not been for this improper preparation of the bride to avoid allegedly breaking her heart, then many families wouldn't have encountered all these problems."[63]

"Some prepare, from the start, all sorts of things as part of the bridal trousseau of their daughter so it would not inferior to that of her cousin, sister or colleague for instance. This is not appropriate. These are wrongful acts, and they bring you the sort of distress for which Allah grants no reward and which doesn't even deserve gratitude."[64]

#25: Taking Others Into Consideration

"When I ask some people, "When two people want to start their lives together, why do you empty the markets in order to prepare for your daughter's bridal trousseau?' They respond, 'Well, we have money and that's why we do it!' Is this reasoning sufficient? Because we have money? No, this reasoning is absolutely insufficient and incorrect. Society includes different types of people; and so, you must behave in a way that allows the girl who doesn't have enough money to get married if so she

---

[63] The Contract Speech dated 1/11/1371 S.H.

[64] The Contract Speech dated 2/9/1378 S.H.

desires. Otherwise, the bridal trousseau which you prepare for your daughter and the dowry which you provide for the bride will shut the doors of marriage in other people's faces. And this approach is neither humane nor Islamic."[65]

#26: The Dowry of the Best Wife in the World ﷺ

"Observe the blessed Prophet's daughter ﷺ, the best of the women of all worlds, Fāṭima al-Zahrā' ﷺ who was the best of the first and last women, such that there wasn't any girl or woman who reached her perfection, honor and greatness. When compared to her ﷺ, all the women of the world – from the first and the last – look like servants or atoms facing the shining sun. Likewise, her husband, the Commander of the Faithful ﷺ, is the best man in the universe. If we were to gather all his virtues and honors, we would find that all the men of the universe do not amount to one of his fingernails. These two manifestations of greatness, beauty and virtue got married, and their wedding furniture included only those few cheap items mentioned and narrated in the books, which were a mat, a piece of palm fiber, a

---

[65] The Contract Speech dated 5/8/1375 S.H.

mattress, a jug and a bowl.⁶⁶ If this furniture was all compiled and evaluated according to the currency used today, its worth wouldn't exceed a few thousand tomans (Iranian currency). They received this dowry amount from the Commander of the Believers, used it to purchase some modest furniture, and carried it to the marital home. We are not saying that in this age, our daughters must bring furniture like that of Fāṭima al-Zahrā'. No; for our daughters are not like Fāṭima al-Zahrā', and we are not like her father and our sons are not like Commander of the Believers, - Fāṭima al-Zahrā''s husband. Who are we compared to them? The difference between us is like that between the land and sky. However, our path is clearly the same, and our direction is the same. So let your furniture be modest, refrain from looking at this and that, don't have a lot of expenses and do not complicate things for those with insufficient means."⁶⁷

"Fāṭima al-Zahrā''s trousseau was of the size which allowed perhaps a person or two to carry it by hand from one house to another. Observe what they bragged about and what their values were. Wasn't

---

⁶⁶ *Biḥār al-Anwār*, part 43, chapter 5, page 94.

⁶⁷ The Contract Speech dated 5/1/1372 S.H.

the Prophet ﷺ capable of providing a lot of furniture?"

"The Prophet ﷺ could have given a mere signal to the Muslims surrounding him who were well-financed, capable and pleading to Allah for an opportunity to grant a gift to the Prophet ﷺ or support him. But he ﷺ didn't. Why didn't he ﷺ do it? The purpose is for you and me to learn from this. We can sit, have a conversation and enjoy ourselves without learning, but what benefit do we reap then? One must not put the doctor's prescription on a shelf and look at it; we must rather apply it to gain its desired benefit. You must commit to a nutritional diet in order to reap its desired advantage. And the things I mentioned act as the nutritional diet for the soul and for the wellbeing of society – the wellbeing of the family – and they must be applied. Carry out your ceremonies with simplicity."[68]

#27: Confronting the Traditions of Jahiliyyah

"Ladies, do not allow them to exaggerate the wedding furniture. The women must not allow it. O brides, you have to confront this issue. Even if your

---
[68] The Contract Speech dated 5/9/1375 S.H.

fathers and mothers wanted it, you must not allow it. What will you do with all these expensive items?"[69]

"The mothers of the brides must be cautious while preparing the wedding furniture. They must not be wasteful or overspending; and they must not say, 'This is our daughter and her heart would be broken.' No, girls are kind; and they did not demand this. So we must not drag them, for no reason, in the direction which makes them believe in the necessity of having beautiful and luxurious preparations."[70]

"The girls who want to prepare for the wedding furniture or purchase items that are relevant to the ceremony must not set foot in expensive shops in places here and there – whose names I don't want to mention, but I know where they are, as they are famous for their high prices. They should rather go to places that are not famous for their high prices. They should not take the poor groom to such places in order to purchase the furniture for the wedding

---

[69] The Contract Speech dated 23/9/1373 S.H.

[70] The Contract Speech dated 16/11/1379 S.H.

and marriage ceremony. Unfortunately, such things do happen."[71]

---

[71] The Contract Speech dated 19/3/1372 S.H.

Chapter Two

The Blessings and Benefits of Marriage

#28: Marriage is the Tranquility of the Soul

Marriage is considered a factor which establishes spiritual tranquility and comfort within the man and the woman, and that's why we find that each is incomplete without the other. For, in reality, they form a complementary entity, such that each of them is supported by his partner. Allah ﷻ says:

And of His signs is that He created for you mates from your own selves that you may take comfort in them, and He ordained affection and mercy between you. There are indeed signs in that for a people who reflect[72]

His Eminence, Imām Khamenei says:

"When the husband and wife finish their daily errands, or meet in the middle of the day and check in with one another, each expects that the other person has managed to make the household a joyful and lively space that does away with weariness. And this expectation is on point. If it's within your

---

[72] Sūrat al-Rūm, verse 21.

capacity, then go ahead and do that; life will be pleasant."[73]

The human being searches amidst the unstable environment, which arises from the mandatory confrontations of life, for refuge. If, amid this instability, there were two spouses who resort to each other, then the husband will resort to his wife and the wife to her husband.

During his lifetime, a man needs moments of tranquility in order to proceed in his journey. When would that moment be? It is during the time he spends in an environment filled with love and familial tenderness, with his affectionate wife along whom he feels as one being. The moment he meets his wife is that moment of comfort and tranquility."[74]

"Amidst her busy life, a woman encounters dilemmas and instabilities, whether she is occupied outside her home with diverse activities such as political, social and other events, or inside her home where her responsibilities are not less substantial than the former. When the woman faces a few problems along

---

[73] The Contract Speech dated 24/1/1378 S.H.

[74] The Contract Speech dated 6/6/1381 S.H.

the way, and due to her sensitive nature, she becomes in need for tranquility, comfort and someone trustworthy to rely on. This person is none other than her husband."[75]

#29: Sharing Concerns is Truly Supportive

"True support for the other person lies in relieving him from all the distress that befalls his heart. Every person is exposed to distress on his journey, where he is afflicted with distress, problems, hesitations or confusion. In these cases, each of the spouses should swiftly support the other in order to relieve him from the distress that befalls his heart, guide him so he may rectify his wrongs or prevent him from committing mistakes."

#30: Spouses are Adornments for one Another

Just as the Qurʾān clarifies the fact that each of the man and woman is a factor of stability for the other, it also emphasizes them being adornments for one another.

---

[75] The Contract Speech dated 6/6/1381 S.H.

Allah says:

⟨*They are a garment for you, and you are a garment for them*⟩[76]

The word garment, in this context, has three meanings:

One of its meanings is "adornment," whereby a woman is an adornment for her husband in the same way a garment is considered as an adornment for him; and the same thing goes for the man in regards to his wife.

Another meaning for the verse is that marriage shields men and women from deviation.

And the third meaning is that both men and women act as a cover for one another.

#31: Home of Solace and Joy

In addition to being a source of tranquility and adornment for each other, each of the spouses is a factor of solace and pleasure for his partner. And the best case, here, would be if the household is truly as

---

[76] Sūrat al-Baqara, verse 187.

Islam willed it to be, and the behavior of both spouses is in line with its teachings.

This is why the blessed Prophet ﷺ says:

"A Muslim man has not benefitted from anything after Islam better than a Muslim wife who pleases him when he looks at her."[77]

It is narrated that a man came to the blessed Prophet ﷺ and told him that his wife treats him as mentioned above, bringing joy to his heart and removing all exhaustion and weariness. The Prophet ﷺ then said:

"The best of your women is the easygoing, gentle and agreeable one who, if her husband gets angry, doesn't sleep before he is pleased, and who preserves her husband in his absence. She is one of Allah's agents, and Allah's agents are never disappointed."[78]

The Guardian of the affairs of the Muslims, Sayyid Ali Khamenei, says, "Marriage and stability within a

---

[77] *Wasā'il al-Shī'a*, part 14, page 230.

[78] *Jāmi' Aḥādīth al-Shī'a Ḥadīth*, part 20, page 38, *ḥadīth* no. 130, 131, 132.

family are one of the important opportunities in life, for they are a means of reassurance, psychological well-being, vitality, stress relief, and sharing troubles. They are a necessity that lasts an entire lifetime.

And regardless of man's creational need - that is the sexual instinct-, giving birth and becoming parents are also of the great pleasures in this world. You notice that, in regards to both parties, marriage is a blessed thing and quite a beneficial phenomenon. The most significant benefit that is anticipated from marriage is the establishment of a family. As for the rest of the matters, they are secondary and come in second place, or they reinforce the primary issue, such as giving birth and satisfying the human instincts. These all come in second place, and creating a family comes first."[79]

"The foundations of the world are rooted in marriage. The transmission of civilizations and cultures, and the stability and independence of societies, whether politically or otherwise, also come

---

[79] The Contract Speech dated 9/12/1380 S.H.

about through marriage. And marriage has many other blessings."[80]

#32: An Opportunity to Reclaim Vitality

Sayyid Khamenei says,

"Within a family, a man and a woman – who live as spouses - can regain their vitality and prepare themselves to resume their journey. You know that life is a struggle. Life, in its entirety, is but a long struggle. It is a battle with natural forces, social obstacles, and the self. A human being is in a constant state of battle, just as the body is in battle against harm. When the body is capable of fighting, this implies its well-being. This battle must certainly be rightful and logical. This battle of direction, behavior, and means, sometimes requires a break and at other times muscular strength. On this journey and movement, the station of restfulness will undoubtedly be the family."[81]

---

[80] The Contract Speech dated 26/1/1377 S.H.

[81] The Contract Speech dated 8/3/1380 S.H.

#33: Establishing a Family

Establishing a family is, in itself, quite a significant matter, and it holds – in Islam – incalculable dimensions and uncountable benefits. When compared to this matter, the satisfaction of the instinct seems trivial, though it is required in its proper channel and in the way intended by Allah.

Sayyid Khamenei says,

"The issue of marriage and establishing a family is quite important in the sacred Sharia and has multiple benefits. However, the most significant benefit and purpose of marriage is the establishment of a family. This marital bond and formation of a new unit are the very reasons behind the comfort experienced by a man and woman, and behind the perfection and completion of both characters. Without this, there would be a lack within both the man and the woman. All other matters are secondary to this one. If this union is well and stable, then it will have an impact on the future and present of society."[82]

---

[82] The Contract Speech dated 10/2/1376 S.H.

The Blessings and Benefits of Marriage

"In reality, marriage is the gateway to establishing a family, and establishing a family is the foundation for all social and human education."[83]

"The core of marriage lies in the connection and relationship between a young man and woman, and in the establishment of a family. This is the extent of it: that the young man and woman meet each other, then the marriage contract is enacted according to the Sharia, and they become husband and wife. Thereby, a new unity is created, and a family is formed. The sacred Legislator loves the sound Muslim family. Establishing a family entails a lot of blessings which fulfill the needs of the husband and wife and carry on with human diversity.

"The objective of forming a family and creating a new unity is – by itself – more important than anything else. The basis of a man and a woman's creation is in their living together within one entity and creating a comfortable and worry-free unit in which one's needs are fulfilled. If this doesn't happen, then there is a significant lack in the basics of life."[84]

---

[83] The Contract Speech dated 18/5/1374 S.H.

[84] The Contract Speech dated 16/5/1379 S.H.

Refinement of the Human Soul

Of the important benefits of marriage is that it is a powerful and supportive factor in the Islamic program of self-refinement, its adornment with virtuous morals and abandonment of vicious ones.

The blessed Prophet says,

"When any man marries in his youth, his devil cries out, 'Woe to him! He has protected his religion from me.'"[85]

A narration states the following:

"If a servant marries, he completes half his religion, may he fear Allah in his other half."[86]

And it is narrated:

"Whoever marries has been given half of worship."[87]

---

[85] *Mīzān al-Ḥikma, ḥadīth* 7805.

[86] *Mīzān al-Ḥikma, ḥadīth* 7807.

[87] *Mīzān al-Ḥikma, ḥadīth* 7808.

Imām al-Ṣādiq says,

"Two cycles of prayer (rakaʿāt) performed by a married man are better than a night of worship and a day of fasting performed by an unmarried man."[88]

And there is a narration about the sleep of a married man and the bounties granted to him by Allah. The Prophet says,

"The married man who is asleep is better, in regards to Allah, than the unmarried man who worships and fasts."[89]

#34: Entering Paradise

Certainly, if man refines himself he enters Paradise, pleases his Lord and angers his and Allah's enemy.

Sayyid Khamenei says,

"Marriage and choosing a spouse sometimes affect a person's fate. A lot of women drive their husbands into Paradise, and a lot of husbands drive their wives into Paradise. The opposite is true as well. If the

---

[88] *Mīzān al-Ḥikma*, ḥadīth 7810.

[89] *Mīzān al-Ḥikma*, ḥadīth 7812.

husband and wife realize the value of the family and take care of it, then they will live in security and comfort. The human perfection of the man and woman will be achieved within a successful marriage."[90]

"Sometimes the man reaches a crossroads in his life where he has to choose between this worldly life and the right path, trustworthiness, and honesty. He has to choose between them. Here, the woman can guide him towards either the first or the second road, and vice versa. The husbands can have this impact on the lives of their wives as well. Attempt to have this relationship where you encourage each other to be religious and take the Godly and Islamic road and the path of truth, trustworthiness, honesty, and the prevention of deviation."[91]

"During the difficult period and years of opposition, in addition to the years of the revolution, many women drove their husbands into Paradise through patience and cooperation. The men went out to different battlefronts and endured hardships, and the women suffered from fear, loneliness, and alienation;

---

[90] The Contract Speech dated 10/2/1375 S.H.

[91] The Contract Speech dated 21/12/1379 S.H.

The Blessings and Benefits of Marriage

however, they never uttered a word of complaint. They rather encouraged their husbands and drove them into Paradise although they could have caused their husbands to regret going to the battlefront and proceeding with the battle. They could've done that, but they didn't. They didn't reveal their weariness.

Similarly, there are men who drove their wives into Paradise, and they guided, supported and cooperated with them in a way that caused these women to take the path of Allah. There are also women who did the opposite, where they drove their husbands into Hell, and there are men who drove their wives into Hell.

You must cooperate and seek to make one another from the people of Paradise, and you must delight each other and support each other in gaining knowledge, perfection, piety and simplicity of living."[92]

"There are plenty of women who make their husbands of the people of Paradise, and plenty of men who make their wives truly happy. The contrary exists as well. There may be good men who are driven by their women into Hell and good

---

[92] The Contract Speech dated 23/12/1379 S.H.

women who are driven by their husbands into Hell. If both men and women are attentive to act upon good advice, joint work, and religion and ethics within the household, and their practical application is clearer than their verbal claims, this is how they support one another and their lives will be truly complete, fulfilling and satisfying."[93]

His Eminence says,

"A man can make his wife one of the people of Paradise by guiding and reminding her at the right time, and preventing her from extravagance and deviation. And the opposite case is certainly true as well, that is, the husband can make his wife one of the people of Hell through excessive demands and wrong expectations and approaches.[94]

---

[93] The Contract Speech dated 11/12/1377 S.H.

[94] The Contract Speech dated 9/4/1378 S.H.

Increase in Sustenance

The Almighty says,

‹Marry off those who are single among you and the upright among your male slaves and your female slaves. If they are poor, Allah will enrich them out of His grace, and Allah is all-bounteous, all-knowing›[95]

And the blessed Prophet says, "Take a spouse, for it increases in your sustenance."[96]

And Imām al-Ṣādiq says,

"He who avoids marriage out of fear of poverty has thought ill of Allah, the Exalted and Glorified.

Allah says,

‹If they are poor, Allah will enrich them out of His grace.›[97]

---

[95] Sūrat al-Nūr, verse 32.

[96] *Mīzān al-Ḥikma*, ḥadīth 7813.

[97] *Mīzān al-Ḥikma*, ḥadīth 7817.

And it is narrated that:

"He who avoids marriage out of fear of poverty is not of us."[98]

#35: Being Grateful for the Gift of Marriage

And if marriage has all this importance and all these benefits, must we not thank Allah for the gift of marriage?

His Eminence says:

"During this phase of your life, where you enter into the shared life and founding a family, consider this to be one of the great Divine blessings and show gratitude for it for everything we have is from Allah the Almighty:

❮And whatever blessing you have is from Allah❯[99]

"Knowing these blessings is quite important. There are many blessings that go unnoticed; and some people get married to a good partner and live a happy life, yet remain unaware of the value of this

---

[98] *Mīzān al-Ḥikma*, ḥadīth 7815.

[99] *Biḥār al-Anwār*, part 49, page 269.

blessing. And they, accordingly, get deprived of the divine mercy that results from gratitude. Therefore, one must realize that marriage is a great blessing and contemplate how he will be thankful for it.

"Sometimes a person says with his tongue solely, 'Thank God,' although it does not come from the heart. This is mere worthless wagging of the tongue. However, when one is truly grateful to Allah ﷻ from the bottom of his heart, gratitude has the utmost value.

"It is to know that Allah has blessed him and show genuine gratitude. This is the required gratitude. The purpose of this matter is that when we thank Allah, we should accomplish a certain action or take a certain stand based on this gratitude. And this is a very good thing.

"Now that Allah ﷻ has blessed you with this gift, what will you do with it? Allah ﷻ didn't demand much of us. The only required thing is to treat this blessing properly. This proper behavior has been clarified by the Islamic religion, that is, through family ethics and wisdom. A happy life lies in knowing how to act in this life."[100]

#36: Practical Gratitude

"Gratitude does not lie in merely saying, 'Thank you, my Lord' or performing a prostration of gratitude. Being grateful for a blessing is in knowing the value of this blessing, that is, in knowing that it is a blessing from Allah, benefitting from it and dealing with it in accordance with what pleases Allah. This is the meaning of being grateful for a blessing. For, if you say, 'thanks be to Allah' without having your hearts understand these concepts which you articulate, then this isn't gratitude. Marriage itself is a divine blessing. Allah has given you a good spouse, and you must be grateful for this blessing in the way that befits it."[101]

---

[100] The Contract Speech dated 29/3/1381 S.H.

[101] The Contract Speech dated 16/1/1379 S.H.

Allah ﷻ says in his Noble Book:

❮*O you who have faith! Save yourselves and your families from a Fire whose fuel is people and stones, over which are [assigned] angels, severe and mighty, who do not disobey whatever Allah has commanded them, and carry out what they are commanded*❯[102]

The family is considered the most significant environment in which a person is molded and developed, psychologically and behaviorally; and it will leave its impact on the society he lives in. Despite their various schools, sociologists agree that the family is the foundation of a society, and that if the family is built on sound grounds then the environment within this society will be stable and its pillars will be reinforced. However, if the foundations of the family become feeble, and none of the diverse conditions of its empowerment are met, then life within this society will become unstable and its balance will be lost.

The family is the primary unit from which the body of society is composed. When it is righteous, this

---

[102] Sūrat al-Taḥrīm, verse 6.

body is well, and when it is corrupt, the body falls into disease and decay.

Due to the great importance of this issue, the Guardian of the Muslims Sayyid Ali Khamenei devoted great attention to it.

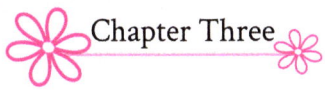
Chapter Three

The Importance of Succeeding in Creating a Family

#37: The Wellbeing of Society Arises from the Wellbeing of the Family

His Eminence Sayyid Ali Khamenei says,

"A person's body is composed of cells, and the corruption, damage, and natural or compulsory illness of the cells means the illness of the body. When this illness spreads, it reaches critical organs in the human body. Similarly, society is composed of cells represented by the family. When these families are sound and their behavior is proper, then society will be sound as well.[103]

If the family structure in a society is strong, and if the spouses respect each other's rights, adopt virtuous morals, are in harmony with one another, face hardships together, and take care of raising their children collaboratively, then society will become virtuous and reach salvation. And if there is a reformer within such a society, he will be able to reform it. Meanwhile, if the family does not exist, then the greatest reformers won't be able to reform society."[104]

---

[103] The Contract Speech dated 8/3/1381 S.H.

[104] The Contract Speech dated 14/6/1372 S.H.

"If the family structure in a certain country is cohesive, then many problems – especially the ethical and moral ones – can be resolved by the blessing of virtuous and cohesive families, or may not even exist in the first place."[105]

"Marriage is one of the great divine blessings, secrets of creation, and reasons behind the continuity, permanence and virtuousness of societies."[106]

#38: The Absence of the Family is the Basis of Psychological Problems

"A society without a family is a troubled society through which cultural and intellectual legacies and ideologies are not easily transferred from one generation to another, and within which the educational process is not carried out smoothly as well. If the family does not exist within a community – or if it is unsteady – then the human being will not receive the best nurture."[107]

---

[105] The Contract Speech dated 2/9/1376 S.H.

[106] The Contract Speech dated 23/12/1379 S.H.

[107] The Contract Speech dated 29/10/1377 S.H.

"If families do not exist, then neither will the virtuous woman nor the virtuous man nor morality; and the good and valuable experiences will not be transferred to the upcoming generation."[108]

"If families do not exist, then there will no longer be a center that instills faith and religious belief."[109]

"In societies where the family structure is weak, nonexistent, less-frequently established, or established on shaky grounds and is in the process of fading away, psychological problems are much more present than in communities where families are stable and the relationship between men and women is narrowed down to one central point."[110]

#39: The Family is the Basis of Education

"A family is a fundamental institution. Its significance lies in educating generations, i.e. developing a sound person at the moral, intellectual and psychological level. This advantage is unparalleled anywhere else and irreplaceable by anything else. Once the family system exists, then

---

[108] The Contract Speech dated 30/3/1379 S.H.

[109] The Contract Speech dated 12/11/1372 S.H.

[110] The Contract Speech dated 21/12/1379 S.H.

every single person of the billion people who exist will be granted two guardians and educators who are devoted specifically to him. Nothing else can take the place of these two educators."[111]

"A family is the safe environment where the father, mother and children can maintain the wellbeing and development of their spirits, intellects, and minds. When the family is weakened, the coming generations will grow unsheltered."[112]

"Man was created for education, guidance, transcendence, and perfection. This only takes place within a safe environment where no complexes are generated, human needs are met, and guidelines are transferred from one generation to another. In such an environment, a person, starting from his childhood, is subject to proper and easy education which is in harmony with his innate nature and delivered by two educators – his father and mother – who are the most merciful people towards him in the entire world."[113]

---

[111] The Contract Speech dated 4/10/1381 S.H.

[112] The Contract Speech dated 18/12/1376 S.H.

[113] The Contract Speech dated 20/5/1376 S.H.

The Importance of Succeeding in Creating a Family

"If the family does not exist within society, then human education will fail, and so will all spiritual human needs. This is how human nature is. Without the family environment and the parents' love, there cannot be a sound, complete education that is free of faults and complexes. The required spiritual transcendence will also be absent. A person will only be wholesome, from the spiritual and emotional aspects, when he is raised within a family. And if the living environment is calm and appropriate, one can be reassured that the children will enjoy emotional and spiritual wellbeing."[114]

"In a family, three types of people are reformed:

First, the men who are the fathers within the family.

Second, the women who are the mothers within that family.

Third, the children who are the succeeding generation in society."[115]

---

[114] The Contract Speech dated 11/5/1374 S.H.

[115] The Contract Speech dated 19/2/1374 S.H.

#40: The Family is the Spring of Culture

"It is due to the blessing that is the family that cultures and civilizations are transferred and their principles and basic elements are preserved for the following generations."[116]

"The basis of marriage and its most significant advantage is creating a family. The reason is that once a wholesome family is established in a society, then that society will become wholesome as well. In that case, the cultural legacy will be transferred properly, and the children will be raised in the best of conditions. Accordingly, communities in which the family system is unstable suffer from ethical and cultural instability."[117]

"If generations want to transfer their mental and intellectual inputs to successive generations, such that the society can benefit from its past, then this can only be done through the family structure and environment. This is where the person's identity and personality are molded for the first time in accordance with the culture of that society. The parents manage to transfer their knowledge, beliefs

---

[116] The Contract Speech dated 26/1/1377 S.H.

[117] The Contract Speech dated 16/1/1377 S.H.

and sacred values to the next generation naturally, indirectly, and without any force or pretension."[118]

#41: The Family is a Person's Comfort

"Islam viewed the family in a proper and authentic manner. Islam perceived the family with great care, regarding it as the basis. The unsteadiness and instability of the family structure are viewed as heinous."[119]

"Family in Islam means the place of comfort and spiritual stability for two human beings, in addition to being a place where they each delight in the company of the other and perfect their personality with the support of the other. Family is that place in which a person finds his psychological stability. The family structure is this important in Islam."[120]

"According to Islam, and as the Qur'ān conveys in various places, the purpose of creating men and women, their coexistence, and eventually their

---

[118] The Contract Speech dated 15/10/1379 S.H.

[119] The Contract Speech dated 15/10/1379 S.H.

[120] The Contract Speech dated 4/10/1374 S.H.

marriage is the stability and serenity of men and women."[121]

This meaning was implied in the Qur'ān in the noble verse:

⟨And made from it its mate, that he might find comfort with her⟩[122]

The term 'comfort' (sakan) is mentioned twice in the Qur'ān, as I recall.[123] Allah ﷻ has created man's mate of his type, that is the woman's husband and the man's wife are of their type. 'That he might find comfort with her' means that so that the person – whether man or woman – can find comfort alongside their spouse."[124]

Stability, comfort, and relief from spiritual turmoil are very important. The fields of life are battlefields where a person is always exposed to turmoil. If

---

[121] The Contract Speech dated 6/9/1376 S.H.

[122] Sūrat al-Aʿrāf, verse 189.

[123] "And of His signs is that He created for you mates from your own selves that you may take comfort in them." Sūrat al-Rūm, verse 21.

[124] Sūrat al-Rūm, verse 21. Editor's Note: this footnote is blank in the original, but the paragraph is also a quotation of one of the Imam's sermons on the theme of marriage.

comfort and stability are realized properly then life will be joyful. The woman and man will be happy, as well as the children, who are born in this house and will grow without any complexes. The groundwork for their happiness will be laid this way."[125]

#42: The More Stable Family Benefits the Most

"Every person, whether man or woman, is exposed to problems in their daily life. They encounter incidents which destroy their soul and lead to their instability. When a person enters his home, this safe environment provides him with vitality and prepares him for a new and upcoming day. A family is quite crucial in organizing the life of the individual, and it must be managed in a progressively better and proper manner."[126]

"The benefit reaped by men and women from a stable household increases their productivity outside the house and enhances its significance and quality."[127]

---

[125] The Contract Speech dated 31/4/1376 S.H.

[126] The Contract Speech dated 29/10/1377 S.H.

[127] The Contract Speech dated 15/12/1379 S.H.

"The opportunity of marriage and stability within a family is one of the significant opportunities in the lives of men and women. It is a means for consolation and sharing one's concerns with a close person, which is considered one of the necessities of life."[128]

#43: The Role of Women and Men in a Family

"The young man and woman must seek to preserve this relationship. This task is not restricted to one of them such that we can say that the second person has to endure all that the first person does. No! Each of them must support the other in making it work."[129]

"It is not right to say that the man or the woman's role is greater. Each has their role in preserving this structure and dual partnership. This role increases gradually afterwards."[130]

"Avoid everything that irritates the household's calmness and leads to depression and negative

---

[128] The Contract Speech dated 9/12/1380 S.H.

[129] The Contract Speech dated 30/7/1376 S.H.

[130] The Contract Speech dated 16/5/1379 S.H.

reactions. The man and woman must be determined to understand and coexist with each other. The bounties that emerge from a family belong to the husband, wife, and children, after all. They do not belong to one party without the other. However, when coldness, instability, or distance takes place – Allah forbid – then the pain will befall both of them."[131]

"The husband and wife have the greatest role in strengthening the family structure through their forgiveness, cooperation, clemency, good morals and, most importantly, love. They have the capacity to make this structure and harmony endure."[132]

#44: Love in Islamic Families

"In the Islamic society, the husband and wife are connected to each other and responsible for one another and for the children and the family."[133]

"Within the Islamic environment, a family is cohesive such that two generations are born, and you can see the grandfather and his grandchildren

---

[131] The Contract Speech dated 6/9/1376 S.H.

[132] The Contract Speech dated 17/11/1379 S.H.

[133] The Contract Speech dated 18/6/1376 S.H.

living together under one roof. How valuable is this? Neither the children get bored of their grandfather, nor does the grandfather wrong his grandchildren; everybody is cooperative."[134]

"In Islamic societies - that is, religious societies - we notice two people who live with each other for a long period of time without getting bored of one another. On the contrary, their love increases; the delight, love and loyalty from one towards the other increase as well. This is the advantage of religiosity and abiding by religious rulings."[135]

"Families persist under Islam and the Islamic culture. You find that the grandfathers, grandmothers, father, mother, grandchildren and great grandchildren transfer their traditions to other generations. The former generation passes its legacy to the successive one in such a way that none are cut off, isolated, or void of emotions."[136]

Many times, a question recurs in the mind of a girl who has reached womanhood, or a boy who has

---

[134] The Contract Speech dated 20/10/1372 S.H.

[135] The Contract Speech dated 2/1/1380 S.H.

[136] The Contract Speech dated 24/5/1374 S.H.

reached manhood. What are the qualifications that must be held by a life partner? Who is the person to whom I should commit and with whom I should stay for the rest of my life?

What are the things that I should take into consideration and be attentive to before and while choosing a spouse, which is a fateful step?

How do I approach marriage without regretting it in the future?

These are all questions that stir in the hearts of young people who are approaching a new life.

 Chapter Four

On Choosing a Spouse

#45: Excessive Idealism

There are some young people who delay marriage, and once you ask them about the reason, they respond by saying, "I haven't found the right person yet." Meanwhile, the truth of the matter lies in the excessive idealism of this person. Below is a piece of advice from His Eminence, Sayyid Ali Khamenei, before starting the discussion on the qualifications upon which one makes the choice of marriage.

His Eminence says,

"Young men and women must not be led astray by excessive idealism in regards to marriage. The ideal person does not exist, and a person cannot get his ideal requirements. Therefore, he must reconcile himself to his life and proceed with his life. If Allah so wills, it will be a happy life which pleases Allah and earns His blessings."[137]

#46: Competence from the Islamic Viewpoint

The general standard of selection is competence. So what does it mean?

---

[137] The Contract Speech dated 6/9/1376 S.H.

His Eminence says,

"It is stipulated in Islamic law that the man and woman must be of equal competence.

The fundamental point in this issue – i.e. the matter of competence – is that competence is faith. This means that they must be faithful, pious, believers in the Islamic principles who act accordingly. Other matters are not important. When the piety and chastity of the girl and boy are ascertained, Allah will take care of the rest of their affairs. That is, the primary factor in this partnership - which is called marriage – in Islam is religion and piety. "A believing man and a believing woman are of equal competence; and a Muslim man and a Muslim woman are of equal competence."[138] This is the Islamic mandate.

It is not a problem if the woman is not at that level yet; she must elevate herself to it. Alternatively, the woman may be superior to the man, in which case he must raise himself to meet her level."[139]

---

[138] *Wasā'il al-Shī'a*, part 20, page 67.

[139] The Contract Speech dated 11/6/1372 S.H.

It is narrated that a man came to Imām al-Ḥasan ﷺ to consult him in regards to giving his daughter in marriage, to which the Imām ﷺ responded,

"Give her to a pious man, for, if he loved her, he would honor her, and if he despised her he wouldn't oppress her."[140]

It was also narrated that Imām 'Alī al-Riḍā ﷺ said,

"If a man asked to marry your daughter, and you were pleased with his religion and morals, then accept his request and do not reject him due to his poverty or destitution."[141] And Allah ﷺ said:

❨If they are poor, Allah will enrich them out of His grace❩[142]

Hereof arose the warning against marrying someone who drinks alcohol, because of his distance from faith, piety and morality.

---

[140] *Mīzān al-Ḥikma*, part 2, page 1184.

[141] *Mīzān al-Ḥikma*, part 2, page 1184.

[142] Sūrat al-Nūr, verse 32.

Such that it was narrated that Imām 'Alī al-Riḍā said:

"Do not give your daughter to someone who drinks alcohol, for if you did, it would be as if you led to fornication."[143]

And a prohibition was mentioned against giving one's daughter to an immoral person, even if he was a blood relative. Someone narrated that he wrote to Abū al-Ḥasan: "I have a relative who asked for my daughter's hand in marriage, and his morals are corrupt. The Imām then said, "Do not marry her off to him if he is immoral."[144]

Likewise, the man must choose a religious and pious woman. The Prophet says,

"A woman is chosen in marriage for four characteristics: her wealth, her religion, her beauty and her lineage. You must marry the woman of religion."[145]

---

[143] *Mīzān al-Ḥikma*, part 2, page 1183.

[144] *Mīzān al-Ḥikma*, part 2, 1183.

[145] *Kanz al-'Ummāl*, 44602.

And Imām al-Bāqir says,

"Indeed, you must marry women of religion."[146]

And His Eminence says,

"If someone gets married for the sake of wealth and beauty, then Allah may and may not give him beauty. However, if he marries in search of piety and chastity, then Allah will give him wealth and beauty as well. Someone may say, 'Beauty is not granted, for one is either beautiful or not.' However, the intended meaning is that once beauty dwells in the eyes and heart, then you will see the other as beautiful, even if he isn't particularly beautiful. Meanwhile, when you are not fond of someone, you will not see him as beautiful no matter how beautiful he actually is."[147]

Now that we've realized the necessity of marriage, the importance of establishing a family, and the risks resulting from its destruction and lack of maintenance, the question that arises is this: How can one maintain happiness in a marriage? And how

---

[146] *Wasā'il al-Shī'a*, part 2, page 21, ḥadīth 14.

[147] The Contract Speech dated 13/10/1377 S.H.

can we preserve the family throughout the entire journey?

His Eminence says,

"In the beginning, one finds everything beautiful. Then, once he gets to know the other person's personality traits, imperfections and weaknesses gradually appear. This must not lead to coldness within the relationship; reconciliation must rather take place in spite of these shortcomings. At the end of the day, the ideal and flawless man does not exist in any region of the world, and neither does the ideal and flawless woman."[148]

---

[148] The Contract Speech dated 24/1/1378 S.H.

Chapter Five

The Secret to a Happy Marriage

#47: Religiosity is the Secret to Family Survival

The Guardian of the Muslims, Sayyid Ali Khamenei, says,

"The Islamic regulations in regards to the establishment, formation, and preservation of the family must be followed in order for it to last and persist. Thus, you see that in religious families where the husband and wife abide by these regulations, they live together for many years, and the love between them remains such that it becomes difficult to separate them, given their adoration of one another. This love is that governs the family structure; this is why Islam gave it so much importance."[149]

"If the Islamic approach is promoted, then family cohesiveness will increase, as was the case in the past – not during the unfortunate Bahlawi period, but rather in the days when people's faith was intact, complete and untainted. During that time, family cohesiveness was more widespread, friendship between the husband and wife was stronger, and children were brought up in a safe and

---
[149] The Contract Speech dated 23/12/1379 S.H.

secure environment. And now this is the road to be taken. Families that abide by the Islamic regulations will most likely be better, stronger and more cohesive; and their environment will be safer for children."[150]

#48: Love is the Fundamental Issue

His Eminence says,

"If there is love, then the hardships confronted outside the house become easier. Likewise, the difficulties encountered by the woman within the household become easier for her."[151]

"The foundation of marriage is (love). Young men and women must know this, and they must preserve the love that Allah has placed in their hearts."[152]

"This humane relationship is based on love and emotional connection; that is, it is necessary that the husband and wife love each other. It is this love that will make their living together easier. Love's roots

---

[150] The Contract Speech dated 15/1/1378 S.H.

[151] The Contract Speech dated 11/8/1377 S.H.

[152] The Contract Speech dated 17/10/1374 S.H.

are not to be found in money or appearances or such things."[153]

"Love is what strengthens the family, and it is the basis of wellbeing in life. And with love's blessing, a person's difficulties are diminished even in regards to his journey towards Allah. If a person enters through love, all his affairs will be made easy for him and all his problems will be resolved."[154]

"The young man and woman - husband and wife - must love each other, for love is the bond that preserves one for the other, keeps them side by side, and inhibits their separation. Love is a beautiful thing. And if love exists then so does loyalty, and rudeness, distress and betrayal will fade away. When there is love, the atmosphere becomes delightful, good, proper and beautiful."[155]

#49: The Greater the Love, the Better

"No matter how great the love between a man and woman is, it can never be excessive. The context in which it is acceptable for love to grow unbounded is

---

[153] The Contract Speech dated 4/9/1375 S.H.

[154] The Contract Speech dated 30/7/1376 S.H.

[155] The Contract Speech dated 24/9/1376 S.H.

that between a husband and wife. The more they love each other, the better, and love itself creates trust.

Love between a husband and wife is a sort of divine love and it's of the good kinds of love. And so, the more it increases the better.

The husband and wife must love each other; this is the foundation of happiness. Happiness lies in loving each other."[156]

"When there is love, thorns turn into flowers. And if there was something unpleasant about the partner, then – in the presence of love – this unpleasant thing will lose its sparkle completely; love covers all faults."[157]

#50: Taking Care of one Another

"The husband and wife must love one another. Refrain from doing things that reduce this love. Beware of behaving in a way that triggers reproach and aversion between you. Look closely into the things that significantly irritate the husband or wife

---

[156] The Contract Speech dated 19/1/1377 S.H.

[157] The Contract Speech dated 15/1/1378 S.H.

and avoid them. Some people do not take this into consideration. Suppose, for example, that the woman detests a certain habit of the man, and he meets this with indifference and keeps repeating this habit. This isn't right!

The same goes for women. For instance, there are some women who choose their personal desires (such as purchasing a certain item or going to a certain place) over their husband's comfort and stability. Why is this necessary?

You two are the core of the matter. And everything else is secondary. Take care of one another and be empathetic with each other."[158]

If a conflict arises – Allah forbid – then it must be dissolved and eliminated through love. Simple words must not be constantly exaggerated and magnified. This should not happen."[159]

"If the husband and wife do not take care of each other's feelings, and absence of love starts appearing on one side, then it will certainly transfer to the

---

[158] The Contract Speech dated 24/9/1371 S.H.

[159] The Contract Speech dated 24/9/1376 S.H.

other. The absence of love is contagious. And so, this is how things unfold. Therefore, do not allow for this to happen. Each of you must strive and make efforts; this is a fundamental matter."[160]

#51: Love is Not an Order

"Love is not an injunction, order or recommendation. It is totally up to you! You can increase the love in your partner's heart day after day. How? Through good morals, proper behavior and being loyal and affectionate to your partner."[161]

"If the wife wants to be loved by her husband then she must make efforts and strive to attain that. Likewise, if the man wants to be loved by his wife, then he must strive and seek it out. Love is pursuit and innovation."[162]

"Love will persist when both parties respect the other's rights and do not violate them; that is, when each of the spouses - who are partners and cohabitants - aims at occupying a solid and powerful position in the heart and mind of the other.

---

[160] The Contract Speech dated 16/5/1379 S.H.

[161] The Contract Speech dated 30/7/1376 S.H.

[162] The Contract Speech dated 19/1/1377 S.H.

This power is a moral power, i.e. a heartfelt connection between the husband and wife.

This is the purpose for which rights in Islam were stipulated."[163]

"If you want love to last, rather than demanding it from the other person, call upon your hearts to flow, more intensely, with love day after day. Love naturally summons love."[164]

#52: Love and Self-Love

"The term 'love' is being misused today. This state which they allege is love is not true love; rather, it is a state of sexual arousal that is manifested in a specific way, and can happen multiple times yet is rendered worthless. The thing which has real value is that deep and honest divine love which is accompanied by a mutual sense of responsibility between the young man and woman, whereby they believe that they are a singular entity in pursuit of a singular goal. This is the love upon which a family is founded."[165]

---

[163] The Contract Speech dated 11/12/1377 S.H.

[164] The Contract Speech dated 19/7/1379 S.H.

[165] The Contract Speech dated 15/10/1379 S.H.

"Love and adoration that do not stand on humane premises, and rather result from appearances and fleeting desires, have no base or foundation.

As for love which is built on the humane grounds set up by Allah ﷻ – especially if it's in line with the recommended conditions that must be followed in an Islamic marriage – it increases day after day."[166]

#53: Mutual Respect

Another beneficial factor in the permanence of the marriage and family strength is mutual respect.

His Eminence says,

"A husband and wife must respect one another – not pretentiously or formally, but rather genuinely."[167]

"For example, respect doesn't lie in them calling each other by titles and polite expressions; it is rather present when each of the spouses carries, within his heart, respect for the other. Preserve this respect within your hearts and maintain sanctity for one another. This is crucial in managing life's

---

[166] The Contract Speech dated 2/1/1380 S.H.

[167] The Contract Speech dated 2/1/1380 S.H.

affairs. There shouldn't be any offense, degradation or humiliation between a husband and wife."[168]

#54: Degrading the Wife is the Beginning of the Family's Destruction

"Oppression, discrimination, and offensiveness are all wrongful acts, irrespective of the circumstances. If a man, for instance, is one of the most perfect men in the world, and his wife – from an academic and cultural viewpoint – is illiterate, or comes from an inferior family, he –doesn't have the slightest right to insult or oppress her. A woman is who she is, and a man doesn't have the right to direct even the smallest insult in her way. This certainly is not limited to us; those well-dressed and perfumed Europeans oppress women – sometimes – even more than our own societies do.

A man doesn't have the right to be rude to his wife even if he is superior to her. And the same goes for a woman. If a woman is well-educated and decides to get married to a working man, she doesn't have the right to offend him. The man is still the support system she must rely on and whose moral state she must preserve in such a way that can support her.

---

[168] The Contract Speech dated 19/9/1371 S.H.

This is the intact family. And if you build a family on these premises, then you must know that you will have guaranteed one of the fundamental pillars of your happiness."[169]

#55: Building Trust

His Eminence says,

"Maintaining love between the husband and wife nurtures trust between them. Whenever trust exists, love is fortified and affability arises."[170]

"The basis of love is trust, and if trust fades away between the husband and wife then love will gradually fade as well. It is crucial that you trust one another.[171] And if you want to increase the other person's love for you, then be loyal to them and earn their trust."

"The absence of trust between the husband and wife is one of the factors that utterly destroys love within a family."[172]

---

[169] The Contract Speech dated 22/1/1378 S.H.

[170] The Contract Speech dated 28/9/1374 S.H.

[171] The Contract Speech dated 19/1/1377 S.H.

[172] The Contract Speech dated 19/7/1379 S.H.

"The necessary groundwork for love must be set. This essential groundwork lies in the woman's attempt to earn the man's trust, and the man's attempt to earn the woman's trust. If mutual trust arises between them and each believes in the other's loyalty, then their love will increase."[173]

"Loyalty is quite significant. If the wife feels her husband's loyalty towards her, and the husband also feels his wife's loyalty towards him, then this – in itself – brings love. Thence, the family will become stable, and this strong entity will persist for many years to come."[174]

"Nevertheless, if the husband or wife feels that their partner's heart is attached to another person, or that they are dishonest with them or being two-faced, or that the intimacy between them isn't present, then the love between them will weaken regardless of its initial intensity."[175]

---

[173] The Contract Speech dated 22/9/1379 S.H.

[174] The Contract Speech dated 30/7/1376 S.H.

[175] The Contract Speech dated 21/12/1379 S.H.

#56: Love's Requirements

"Love is Allah's gift to you. The capital which Allah gifts to the young man or woman at the beginning of marriage mutual love between them. And this must be preserved.

Your partner's love towards you is connected to your behavior with them. For, if you want their love for you to last then you should behave affectionately towards them. Thus, what a person should do to show his love becomes clear. He must be loyal, and must show honesty, sincerity, love and cooperation, and he must not raise his expectations. These are the things that create love, and this is the responsibility of each party towards the other. There must be love and cooperation within the marital life, and there mustn't be a lot of objections and demands."[176]

#57: Trust is Not a Contractual Agreement

"Trust is not a contractual matter – i.e. I trust you and you trust me. This is not the case. Trust must rather be earned by good treatment, abiding by ethics and manners, and respecting the religious boundaries and regulations."[177]

---

[176] The Contract Speech dated 19/12/1376 S.H.

[177] The Contract Speech dated 10/2/1375 S.H.

"Distrust nips love in the bud. Do not allow it to exist. The feeling of disloyalty is like leprosy; it devours love and destroys it."[178]

"If the wife feels that her husbands is lying to her, or the husband feels that his wife is lying to him, or either of them feels that the other is being dishonest in showing his love, then this will enfeeble the foundation of their love. If you want to perpetuate the love between you, then you must preserve the trust between you. And if you want to perpetuate your shared life, then you must maintain your love."[179]

#58: Mutual Understanding and Consideration

"The man must understand the woman's needs and emotions; he must not neglect her and claim himself to be the unbridled choice-maker of the household. The husband and wife are two individuals who are partners and friends; each has an intellectual and spiritual aspect. The man must support the woman in catching up with the developments of society."[180]

---

[178] The Contract Speech dated 16/11/1379 S.H.

[179] The Contract Speech dated 6/6/1381 S.H.

[180] The Contract Speech dated 10/2/1375 S.H.

"Islam has taken measures within the family by which internal conflicts get automatically resolved. It demands that the man and woman be considerate. And if this consideration takes place, then no family will ever disintegrate or be eliminated, since the disintegration of families is mainly caused by inconsiderateness. The man who doesn't know how to be considerate, the woman who doesn't behave reasonably, and he who uses violence and excessive harshness - which becomes unbearable for the woman - are all off course. A man's harshness is wrong, and so is a woman's stubbornness. If one time a man who isn't harsh in his temperament commits a mistake, the woman mustn't be difficult. They must be considerate and harmonious. Thence, no family will ever disintegrate; it will rather last forever."[181]

#59: Sexual Chastity

"Islam made the sexual instinct the foundation for establishing a family; that is, it is a means through which the family is strengthened. What does this mean? It means that if the man and woman are chaste, religious, pious, and refrain from sin in regards to the sexual instinct – as per the Islamic

---

[181] The Contract Speech dated 20/11/1375 S.H.

law – then their need for one another will increase. And if this need increases, then this family which is established by the man and woman will be more cohesive."[182]

"Islam aspires to preserve this pillar within families and emphasizes that people are not to satiate this instinct outside the family domain so that they don't become indifferent and careless towards their families. For this reason, Islam has shut the doors that lead to that."[183]

#60: Chastity and the Ḥijāb: The Stronghold of the Family

"The issues of the maḥram[184], the foreigner, the ḥijāb, and the permission and prohibition of the gaze and unhealthy and harmful relationships have all been widely emphasized by Islam. These things are not applied in some countries and regions that are far from Islam.

---

[182] The Contract Speech dated 9/12/1380 S.H.

[183] The Contract Speech dated 18/12/1376 S.H.

[184] English translator's note: a member of one's family with whom marriage is illegal in Islam.

These matters, though they involve constraints for women, have been stipulated and reinforced by the sacred Legislator for the preservation of the family and the stability of this significant entity. Any person who ponders and contemplates this issue will realize the great wisdom behind it."[185]

"When you observe the issues of the mahrams, foreigners, non-mixing between genders and its likes in Islam, you will realize that they are not regressive; they are rather of the most sensitive human issues. Of the most significant of these issues is preserving the cohesiveness of families, because the husband and wife will be loyal towards one another and will not envy one another. And this is quite a crucial matter."[186]

"This hijāb that is stipulated by Islam, along with its prohibition of the unlawful gaze and considering such relationships prohibited are all for the sake of focusing your love and hearts on one point, whether you are men or women."[187]

---

[185] The Contract Speech dated 11/12/1377 S.H.

[186] The Contract Speech dated 15/10/1379 S.H.

[187] The Contract Speech dated 30/1/1379 S.H.

"The things you observe in Islam such as the hijab, covering up, non-mixing between genders and its likes – and which some narrow-minded and short-sighted people claim to be superficial – are in fact very deep issues. Their purpose is the cohesiveness of the family, the steadiness of the spouses' hearts, and the stability of the household. They have been stipulated for this purpose. The issues that have been raised by Islam and Islamic jurisprudence such as mahrams and non-mahrams and the prohibitions which say, 'don't look,' 'don't have a relationship,' 'don't shake hands', 'don't laugh,' don't wear makeup' and 'don't beautify yourself in front of others' all have one aim. This aim – if followed – is to render your entity and established family cohesive and problem-free. The man and woman will feel that the fate of one of them is connected to the fate of the other and to that of the family. The woman will not, thus, feel restrained by the household, and the man will not feel annoyed by the woman and household."[188]

"Islam's emphasis on lowering the gaze, the unlawfulness of gazing at a foreigner and guiding the man and woman in a certain way results from

---

[188] The Contract Speech dated 15/12/1379 S.H.

the fact that if a man's eye stays towards a certain direction, then part of his wife's share will go to that direction. And there is no difference in regards to this matter between a man and a woman; either way, part of one's share will go to that direction. And when that share decreases, then love weakens and the family foundations quiver. Thence, you will lose that which benefits you and gain that which harms you – and which you had falsely believed to have attained."[189]

#61: The Philosophy of the Ḥijab and Chastity

"When Islam and the Qur'ānic verses speak of the ḥijab, and when the relationship between man and woman is codified, then this will be in the advantage of the people themselves: the families, the women who don't want to lose their husbands, and the young men who don't want to lose their beloved wives. This is unattainable without committing to the ḥijab. The Qur'ānic verses have proven to be wise and profound."[190]

---

[189] The Contract Speech dated 17/2/1375 S.H.

[190] The Contract Speech dated 11/5/1375 S.H.

"The distinction between a foreigner and non-foreigner, and the ḥijab and covering of the woman, and Allah's ﷻ saying,

❁Tell the faithful men to cast down their looks and to guard their private parts❁[191]

which means do not open your eyes for every view, and do not look at everything lest you get attracted to everything; why does all this exist? All this is so that the husband and wife remain loyal and empathetic towards each other. A man and woman, in the corrupt societies of the world, mix with the other sex wherever they go, and act however they desire. What is the importance of the family from their viewpoint? It has no importance! And they call this freedom! If this is freedom, then it is one of the greatest catastrophes which has befallen humanity.

"A man who has no restraint and can lean towards women as he wishes without any shielding boundary, and a woman who is not adorned with modesty, chastity, and the humane ḥijab and has no shield do not hold for their partners any respect or significance. In Islam, the man and woman are

---

[191] Sūrat al-Nūr, verse 30.

responsible for one another, love one another, and need one another. Why does this long chain of regulations exist in regards to the marital life?

"All these regulations aim at maintaining the cohesiveness of the family and keeping the spouses together, whereby none of them betrays the other."[192]

#62: Enjoin one Another to the Truth and Patience

"Unity of the heart and cooperation mean that you protect each other on the path towards Allah. Enjoin one another to be follow the truth and be patient. If the lady of the house sees that her husband is at risk of deviation, by – for instance – carrying out an illegal transaction, following a wrongful course, gaining an unlawful income, or making wicked friendships, then she is the first person who must safeguard him against all this. Likewise, if the husband feels that his wife has erred, then he must be the first to protect her. Certainly, protection is carried out through love, kind words, sound reasoning, and wise behavior rather than immorality, 'pouting,' and the like. Each must watch

---

[192] The Contract Speech dated 12/9/1377 S.H.

over the other person to make sure that he doesn't stray from the righteous path."[193]

#63: Moral Supervision is a Form of Care

"The most important kind of support for the partner is working on preserving his religiosity. Take care that your partner isn't committing any religious mistakes. This watchfulness is not intended to be a form of censorship and surveillance. It is rather looking after someone in a moral, empathetic, compassionate, and caring manner. If you see that your partner has committed a mistake, then you must resolve and eliminate this mistake through a gentle and wise approach."[194]

#64: Triggering Jealousy and Envy

"Do not trigger each other's envy and jealousy:

I always advise young men: during your interactions with non-mahrams or even mahrams– do not do anything or speak in a way that triggers your wives' envy. And I advise women as well to refrain from doing anything or speaking with non- mahrams in a way that arouses their husbands' jealousy and envy.

---

[193] The Contract Speech dated 21/8/1379 S.H.

[194] The Contract Speech dated 3/8/1379 S.H.

This envy brings about distrust, weakens the foundations of love, and nips it in the bud."[195]

#65: Safeguarding Marital Secrets

"The husband and wife must safeguard each other's secrets. The wife must not disclose her husband's secrets in front of others. And the same goes for the man. He must not, for example, wander and disclose his wife's secrets in a public gathering or during a visit. Beware of this. Safeguard each other's secrets, so that your life remains beautiful and cohesive – if so Allah wills."[196]

#66: Mutual Harmony

A flawless person doesn't exist!

"If you recognize a flaw in your partner which must be tolerated – and there's no such thing as a flawless person – then tolerate it; he must be, simultaneously, tolerating one of your flaws as well. A Person doesn't recognize his own flaws; he rather notices others'. This is why one must endure. If the flaw is fixable, then fix it. Otherwise, adapt to it."[197]

---

[195] The Contract Speech dated 10/9/1379 S.H.

[196] The Contract Speech dated 24/1/1378 S.H.

[197] The Contract Speech dated 9/4/1378 S.H.

"In the past, it was said that the woman was the one who had to get along with her husband; it's as if they hadn't recognized any role for the man in the process of getting along with his wife. No! Islam doesn't say that. Islam rather says that the young man and woman must both get along, come to an agreement, and plan to manage their family life in a proper, complete, and calm manner which is accompanied by mutual love and adoration. And they must continue with this approach and preserve it. If this is carried out, if Allah wills – and it's not difficult within an Islamic upbringing – then this family will be wholesome from the Islamic viewpoint."[198]

#67: Imām Khomeini: "Go and Get Along"

"I once went to Imām Khomeini, and he was about to marry a couple. As soon as he saw me, he said, 'Come and be a party in the contract.' Contrary to what I used to do in regards to speaking at length and in detail, he would just read the marriage formula at first and then speak briefly. And I noticed that after reading the formula of the contract, he looked at the young man and woman and told them, 'Go and get along.' I thought about it and realized

---

[198] The Contract Speech dated 11/5/1374 S.H.

that despite all that we say, Imām Khomeini has summarized everything in this phrase: 'Go and get along.'"[199]

#68: What does Harmony mean?

"Aim your efforts in all the stages of your lives – especially during the first four or five years – at getting along with each other. Do not adopt the attitude by which once your partner behaves in a way that implies lack of harmony, you meet them by acting similarly. No!

"Get along. And if you see that your partner is being disagreeable, then be agreeable yourself. This is one of the areas in which bargaining and compromising are good."[200]

"What does harmony mean? Does it mean that the woman recognizes her ideal image in this man before she gets along with him, or that the man recognizes his ideal image in this woman who represents his utmost ambition before getting along with her? In such a case, if deviation – no matter

---

[199] The Contract Speech dated 20/4/1370 S.H.

[200] The Contract Speech dated 31/4/1376 S.H.

The Secret to a Happy Marriage

how minor - is detected here or there, then it is unacceptable; is this the meaning of harmony?

"No! If this was the case, then harmony takes place naturally and independently of your will. When it's said that you must get along, this means that you must adapt to the current circumstances or the circumstances that have come up; this is the meaning of harmony. Some issues may come up in life whereby the spouses - who aren't well-acquainted with one another or belong to different cultures or different traditions – may not feel harmonious with one another at first. This would not be at the very the beginning of the marriage but after a while.

"Would it be acceptable for the man or woman to neglect one another and say, 'He no longer suits me?!'

"No! You must adapt yourself to this situation. If it is fixable, then fix it. And if not, then you must adapt to it."[201]

---

[201] The Contract Speech dated 16/1/1379 S.H.

"Harmony within the household is an obligation. The man and woman must not be under the impression that their demands are unquestionable. This is not how things go. Things must rather be built on harmony between them; this harmony is crucial. And if you realize that what you seek will not be fulfilled except by compromise, then compromise."[202]

"Harmony, in life, is the basis of its continuity and the source of love and divine blessings. Harmony brings hearts closer together and strengthens relationships."[203]

#69: Understanding the Other Person

"The core of marriage lies in the understanding, affability, and unity shared by two beings. This is, in principle, a natural thing. However, by surrounding marriage with rules, etiquettes, and regulations, Islam has granted it perpetuity and blessing. 'The husband and wife must perceive and understand one another.' This is a European expression, but a good one. It means that each must realize the pain and needs of the other person, and treat him with

---

[202] The Contract Speech dated 9/4/1378 S.H.

[203] The Contract Speech dated 19/11/1377 S.H.

forgiveness. This is what is called 'perception'. In other words, there must be mutual understanding and perception in life. And this increases love."[204]

#70: Refraining from Negative Intervention

"The youth must be guided. However, one must not intervene a lot in the particularities of their lives, as this will complicate things."[205]

"It is impermissible for some people to destabilize this strong establishment, whether by intervention, shallowness, or childish attitudes. If these people realize that their intervention ruins the relationship between the husband and wife, then they don't have the right to intervene from that moment onwards."[206]

"If the elders want their children to live happily, then they must provide them with advice and guidance. However, they must not intervene in their affairs; rather, they must let them live their own lives."[207]

---

[204] The Contract Speech dated 31/6/1371 S.H.

[205] The Contract Speech dated 6/9/1376 S.H.

[206] The Contract Speech dated 17/2/1375 S.H.

[207] The Contract Speech dated 18/5/1374 S.H.

Sayyid Ali Khamenei says,

"The elders must not – Allah forbid – approach one of the spouses and criticize the other, or say what disturbs the souls. They must, rather, seek to bring the spouses closer to each other and connect their hearts even further."[208]

"The parents have a great role in creating love. The husband or wife's parents must ensure that the spouses love each other. If they detect something they don't like about the other person, then they must not share it with their son or daughter. They must allow the two to delight more deeply in each other, and give space for their love to grow day after day."[209]

"The fathers and mothers must try to secure the love between the husband and wife – who are their newlywed young children. A conflict may arise, every now and then, in which case the older and more experienced parents shouldn't allow for it to

---

[208] The Contract Speech dated 11/8/1377 S.H.

[209] The Contract Speech dated 31/6/1371 S.H.

result in the coldness of the relationship between the young couple."[210]

---

[210] The Contract Speech dated 9/12/1380 S.H.

Chapter Six

The Western Predicament

#71: The Western Family

The Guardian of the Muslims, Sayyid Ali Khamenei, says,

"It's a given that modern, non-Muslim families, especially in the West, suffer from disintegration and turmoil and are currently disappearing or collapsing, as some sociologists opine.

The severance of the parent-child bond has grown in western countries due to parents' occupation at work and the industrial countries' exhaustion of mothers' nurturing capacities in factories. This has led to the child's isolation from his parents and his enrollment in boarding schools where he would be separated from his parents throughout his childhood years.

This resulted in the deterioration of the emotional and spiritual aspect in the personalities of people in many industrial countries. This led to the disintegration of the family, its disorientation and the separation of its members."

He also says,

"What's witnessed today in western countries are generations without an identity – lost and confused generations – and fathers and mothers who know nothing about their children for years even though they live in the same city. This is to say nothing of family members living in different cities. The family has disintegrated and people live in isolation."[211]

"There is a huge number of unmarried women, as well as unmarried men, in European and American countries, which results in children without parents, street children, and consequently felons. That environment is the criminal environment – as you hear in the news – where a child suddenly commits a murder in a school, street or train by which he kills people. This doesn't happen once or twice, and it doesn't result in killing only one or two people. The age range of the perpetrators is gradually declining. They used to be twenty-year-old youngsters, then became as young as seventeen and sixteen, and now thirteen and fourteen-year-old boys commit crimes in America whereby they murder a human being in cold blood. When a

---

[211] The Contract Speech dated 28/2/1374 S.H.

community reaches this level, it cannot be reconnected and rebuilt afterwards."[212]

#72: The West's Biggest Sin

"One of the west's problems which will gradually destroy it like a termite and expose it to collapse and destruction over time – despite its industrial and scientific advancement – is the issue of neglecting the family. They [Westerners] didn't manage to preserve the family. In the West, the family is alienated, neglected, and degraded."[213]

"One of the biggest mistakes committed by Western civilization against humanity is that it devalued marriage for people and underestimated the issue of creating a family. They dealt with marriage as if it were a garment that they take off at will."[214]

"The foundations of the civilization of countries in which families have been torn apart are, in fact, shaking and will eventually collapse."[215]

---

[212] The Contract Speech dated 9/11/1376 S.H.

[213] The Contract Speech dated 1/12/1374 S.H.

[214] The Contract Speech dated 24/1/1376 S.H.

[215] The Contract Speech dated 9/11/1376 S.H.

#73: Women's Loneliness

"How many women live by themselves? A woman lives by herself in an apartment away from her family, comes back alone at night and wakes up alone in the morning, with no one to keep her company, no husband, no child, no grandchild and no relative to speak to. People, in that social environment, generally live individually and alone. Why is this the case? The answer is that because the family environment is lost and nonexistent in those societies."[216]

"Today, it's unfortunately noticeable that in the West, the family structure is declining and fading away. The impact of this is manifested in the cultural chaos and corruption with which they've been inflicted, and which have been increasing day after day until all they have is lost."[217]

#74: Sexual Freedom and the Collapse of the Family

"In the Western world – especially in America and a few countries in northern Europe – it is well-known that the family structure is extremely unstable. Why

---

[216] The Contract Speech dated 5/8/1375 S.H.

[217] The Contract Speech dated 18/4/1377 S.H.

so? The reason goes back to excessive sexual freedom and moral decay in those regions. When sin is widespread, and the man and woman fulfill their sexual desires outside the family, then this structure is rendered a meaningless imposed formality. That's why men and women are emotionally distant even though they are not separated; they do not love each other."[218]

#75: Moral Decay is the Cause of the Collapse

"If people are left unrestrained, then they will satiate their sexual instinct as they wish. The family is nonexistent, and if it is formed then it is weak, hollow, and prone to threat and destruction such that any storm can uproot it. This is why you notice that wherever there is sexual freedom in the world, the family structure is respectively weakened, for the man and woman do not need a social system to fulfill their sexual instinct.

On the other hand, in all the places where religion reigns and sexual freedom is absent such that everything is restricted to the relationship between

---

[218] The Contract Speech dated 9/12/1380 S.H.

the husband and wife, the family structure is protected."[219]

#76: Artificial Love

"In some countries where science has advanced expediently, people have been compelled to live in way that family members do not interfere in each other's affairs. The father works in a certain place and the mother works elsewhere, and neither of them sees or cooks for the other. Neither of them shows love and empathy to the other, neither of them pleases the other, and they do not share any real connection. If they decide to abide by the recommendations provided by psychologists in regards to children, then they agree on a specific timing during which the father and mother go home and hold a family meeting. In order to hold this family meeting, which takes place naturally in intact families, they create it for themselves artificially. During the meeting, the man or woman keeps looking at their watches to see when the meeting will end, since they have a scheduled appointment at 6 o'clock elsewhere for instance. There's no presence

---

[219] The Contract Speech dated 20/4/1370 S.H.

of a familial atmosphere or meeting, and the children do not experience affability."[220]

#77: Artificial Families

"Families there are unloving. They don't even exist in reality. A man and woman live in the same place yet are separated from each another. There isn't any trace of family gatherings, family love, or deep affability. The man doesn't find himself in need of the woman, nor does the woman find herself in need of the man. They are simply two people living under one roof."[221]

#78: The Age of Marriage

"In Western societies, young people spend their age of vitality and sexual arousal in total freedom. By the time they decide to move towards marry and establish a family, a huge part of their natural desire and instincts will have been extinguished; that longing, love, and adoration that is supposed to be ingrained within the souls of the husband and wife fades or diminished as well."[222]

---

[220] The Contract Speech dated 22/4/1379 S.H.

[221] The Contract Speech dated 2/9/1373 S.H.

[222] The Contract Speech dated 17/11/1379 S.H.

"What's suggested by some people in regards to setting the age of marriage at middle age in accordance with what's being done in the West and Western culture is a mistake. It contradicts with innate human nature and the interests of humanity, and rises from the tendency to satiate sexual desires. Lovers wish to spend their youth in pleasure – as they call it – and a young man commits all sorts of sins; later, after his vitality is gone, his passion is lost, and his sexual desire is extinguished, he decides to start a family.

You notice that this is the case with family life in the West: plenty of divorce and unsuccessful marriages, disloyal men and women, multiple sexual transgressions, and lack of jealousy. This is what family life means over there."[223]

#79: The Collapse of Family Due to Inappropriate Age

"If you look at Western societies today, especially those that have an industrial sector and satellite and electronic communications, you will realize that corruption increases over there day after day. If moral corruption spreads within a society, then that

---

[223] The Contract Speech dated 26/1/1377 S.H.

society will collapse. These afflictions do not strike all at once like an earthquake or a flood; they are rather gradual afflictions. The problem is that they don't have a cure, for these kinds of afflictions are not quickly identified, but rather gradually. This means that only after things hit rock bottom do people start noticing, and by then it will be incurable. Things have, in reality, reached this extremely dangerous phase of decline, and this all goes back to the fact that young men and women do not engage in a successful and stable marriage at an appropriate age. Later, once the family is established, the family atmosphere will be void of love."[224]

"The family structure has been shaken in the West, and there's a delay in the establishment of the family, which quickly collapses as well. Corruption and obscenity increase day after day, and if this worsens, then those societies will be inflicted with severe misfortunes. Such diseases and problems are not detected within five to ten years; they rather leave their mark after many years when society collapses completely and all its scientific, intellectual, and material riches are wasted. This is

---

[224] The Contract Speech dated 23/12/1379 S.H.

what awaits many Western countries in the future."[225]

#80: The Family Conditions in the West

"Observe how European and American communities are troubled and unstable, how they crave stability. Observe how widespread the consumption of sleeping pills and tranquilizers has become. Observe how many young men behave in abnormal ways such as growing their hair long and wearing tight clothes because they are agitated – nay, angry – at the conditions of society. They want to reach stability, but eventually get disappointed. Elderly men and women die in nursing homes and none of their children are with them. Wives don't have a clue about their spouses, as husbands and wives are distant from each other."[226]

"In the West, there are children who don't know who their fathers and mothers are. And a lot of women and men are spouses by name only, spending years without knowing anything about the other person. Few were the women who were at ease until the end of their lives, and who spent their old age

---

[225] The Contract Speech dated 3/8/1379 S.H.

[226] The Contract Speech dated 22/1/1374 S.H.

with their man and under his protection. How many are the men who were at ease knowing that their wives whom they love will not leave them tomorrow and choose to live independently?!"[227]

#81: Will Anyone Listen?

"In America itself, the percentage of widespread corruption in all its forms (moral, sexual, and criminal...) among people is high, even among children.

The press and wise people in Western society are crying out, writing articles, speaking and warning, but no one is listening. This means that there is no cure. When things became corrupt and thirty or forty or fifty years passed like this, these problems could no longer be resolved by warning calls or implementing this policy or that."[228]

"Western societies are not happy. This isn't coming from me. This is rather coming from their intellectuals, their distraught experts, and wise individuals who live within those communities, and not from politicians.

---

[227] The Contract Speech dated 11/5/1375 S.H.

[228] The Contract Speech dated 3/6/1375 S.H.

Why the outcry now? It's because the means for happiness are not available in those societies, for happiness requires stability, comfort, and security."[229]

"People knowledgeable about global thought know that in America – more than any place else – and in European countries as well, the calls of good people and reformers echoed loudly, 'Come on, let's think!' And it is certainly not easy for them to think; and if they do think, it's not easy for them to reach a cure."[230]

#82: The Family and Identity

"Those who seek power in a country or society seize its culture and impose their own culture on its people. One of their strategies is weakening the family; they unfortunately did it in many countries, where men became irresponsible and women immoral."[231]

"The transmission of cultures and civilizations, the preservation of traditions and original elements of a

---

[229] The Contract Speech dated 30/3/1379 S.H.

[230] The Contract Speech dated 9/11/1376 S.H.

[231] The Contract Speech dated 18/12/1376 S.H.

civilization or culture in a certain community, and its transference across successive generations only happens by the blessing of the family. If families do not exist, everything falls apart; You notice the Westerners' attempts of spreading lusts and corruption in Eastern and Islamic countries. Why so?

One of their objectives is that they want to tear apart families in order to weaken the culture within these societies, which gives them the power to control them. As long as a people's culture doesn't weaken, no one will be able to subdue it, silence it, and control it.

The thing that robbed peoples of their capacity to defend themselves and made them captives in the hands of foreigners was loss of the cultural identity. This is facilitated by the destruction of the family in society.

Islam wants us to preserve the family. One of the most significant things in Islam – for the sake of reaching these objectives – is the establishment and preservation of the family."[232]

---

[232] The Contract Speech dated 26/1/1377 S.H.

#83: A Speech on Family

"I delivered a one-hour speech at the United Nations; part of it was related to family. They told me later on that the American TV stations, despite their censorship and distortion of my words, have emphasized this speech, replayed it several times, and explained it. This was solely because it included a sentence on the family. This means that a speech that includes a word on family is for the West today as delightful as fresh cold water. They feel a deficiency in this area.

How many women live their whole lives in loneliness? And how many men live estranged without a companion? How many young people wander aimlessly because they don't have a family? Even if they do have a family, it feels nonexistent."[233]

---

[233] The Contract Speech dated 24/9/1376 S.H.

Chapter Seven

Mutual Rights of the Husband and Wife

Mutual Rights of the Husband and Wife

The Oppression of Women by Society and the Husband

A woman, nowadays, is being oppressed by society and her husband. This oppression isn't restricted to our age, as she was oppressed in the past as well.

If we wanted to see what history says about this, it would take us a long time. Therefore, we will mention a few historical examples to highlight the terrible things that had befallen poor women. In Ecclesiastes (from the distorted Torah), we find: "So I turned my mind to understand, to investigate and to search out wisdom and the scheme of things and to understand the stupidity of wickedness and the madness of folly. I find more bitter than death the woman who is a snare, whose heart is a trap and whose hands are chains."[234]

The text continues:

"I found one upright man among a thousand, but not one upright woman among them all."[235]

---

[234] Editor's note: Ecclesiastes 7:25-26.

[235] Editor's note: Ecclesiastes 7:28.

Most ancient nations believed that a woman's deeds were not accepted by Allah ﷻ. In Greece, she was called an abomination created by the devil. Some Romans and Greeks believed that she didn't have a soul although the man was considered to have an immaterial human soul.

After much discussion, a council discussing women that was held in France in the year 586 CE decided that a woman was a human being, but that she was created to serve man.[236]

Approximately a hundred years ago in England, woman wasn't considered part of human society. You can refer, in this regard, to the books of opinions, beliefs and ethics of religions; you will marvel at their opinions.[237]

In the age of Jahiliyyah, the Arab woman was inferior to any commodity; she didn't inherit nor did

---

[236] Editor's note: This is a frequently repeated but ahistorical myth. "Neither the word 'woman' nor the word 'soul' occurs even once in the decrees… A single bishop queried the meaning of a word. The others felt there was no substance to his problem, and he accepted their views. There was no debate as to whether women are human, much less a decision that they do not have a soul." See Michael Nolan, "The Mysterious Affair at Mâcon: The Bishops and the Souls of Women," in New Blackfriars, 74.876 (1993): 501-507.

[237] Mīzān al-Ḥikma, part 4, page 2868.

she have the right to demand her inheritance because she didn't take part in war. Her marriage decision was to be made by her guardian, and she didn't have the right to object or have a say. Furthermore, the son had the right to prevent his father's widow from remarrying unless she gave back all that she had taken from his father's inheritance. He could go even further by laying his garment on her and claiming that she herself was part of his father's legacy. If he wanted to marry her, he could do it without providing a dowry, or he could marry her off and take her dowry himself. The people of Jahiliyya were known for female infanticide.

And Allah ﷻ referred to this by saying,

❬When the girl buried-alive will be asked for what sin she was killed❭[238]

The ancient Egyptian woman underwent a lot of persecution and humiliation. She was treated with contempt and degradation like servants; she wasn't good enough to do anything save housekeeping and raising children!

---
[238] Sūrat al-Takwīr, verses 8-9.

The ancient Egyptian man would feel joyful when told that his wife had given birth to a boy. Meanwhile, his face would grow dim if he knew that his wife had given birth to a girl.[239]

The ancient Greek woman wasn't better off. In their view, she was nothing more than a creature of the lowest class who was terribly insulted and humiliated in all aspects of social life. As for the positions of honor and dignity within society, they were all dedicated to men."[240]

As for ancient India, a woman was considered a possession owned by the man. They would sacrifice her on the pyre of her deceased husband such that if her husband passed away before her, they would burn her alive with him.[241]

The oppression wasn't restricted to societies, for some philosophers oppressed women through their opinions. [Pierre-Joseph] Proudhon, the socialist philosopher, said that a woman's heart is weaker than men's as much as her mind is weaker.

---

[239] *Al-Mar 'a fil-islām*, page 27.

[240] Abū ʿAlī Mawdūdī, *Kitāb al-Ḥijāb*, page 29.

[241] *Al-Mar 'a fil-islām*, page 31.

The philosopher Rousseau said that a woman was not created for knowledge, wisdom, thinking, art, or politics. She was rather created to be a mother and breastfeed her children.

#84: Modern Society's Oppression of Women

That was the oppression inflicted on women by ancient societies and philosophers. As for the oppression committed by modern societies unto women, it is far more dangerous because it conceals itself behind flashy titles, such as equality, freedom, justice, and human rights.

His Eminence says,

"The arrogant world, which is immersed in ignorance, is mistaken when it believes that the value and worth of a woman lie in beautifying herself in front of men such that reckless eyes can gaze at her, enjoy her, and applaud her. This is what the degenerate Western culture promotes today under the title of women's rights. The Western proposition exposed women to men for their enjoyment such that women become a means of pleasing men. And they call this 'women's freedom'. Is this women's freedom?

Those who claim to safeguard human rights and women's rights within the ignorant, negligent, and deviant Western world are in fact the ones who are oppressing women.

You have to view a woman as a noble human being before it becomes clear to you what her rights, freedom and perfection mean. Look at the woman and her freedom. Perceive her as a fundamental factor in establishing a family.

The oppression inflicted on women by Western culture and the misconception of women in Western culture and literature are unparalleled throughout all of history. Women were oppressed in the past; however, the more general and all-embracing oppression is recent. It resulted from Western culture, which has perceived women as a means for men's pleasure, and called this 'women's freedom.'

Is there any interest in the positive aspects and noble values of a woman? Is there an interest in the delicate emotions, empathy, and sympathetic nature which Allah ﷻ bestowed on women with their maternal nature and nurturing spirit?"[242]

---

[242] *Dawr al-Mar'a fil-Usra*, Markaz al-Imām al-Khumaynī, first floor, 1434 AH – 2003 CE, pages 35-36.

#85: Man's Oppression of Women

All of this relates to the oppression committed by society. As for man's oppression of his wife within the household, His Eminence Sayyid Ali Khamenei says,

"Those people aren't speaking of women's oppression within the social field, for the primary oppression inflicted on women takes place inside the household and at the hands of the husband.

"Perhaps 90% of this oppression is committed by the husband. We must think of a solution to fix this issue. As for the oppression committed by the brother, sister, father and their likes, it isn't pervasive. It's quite rare actually. The most important thing is the familial relationship, particularly that between the man and woman and other such relationships which result in the oppression of women."[243]

#86: Mutual Rights

The issue of rights occupies a large space and has great significance in Islam.

---

[243] *Mīzān al-Ḥikma*, pages 36-37

Imām al-Riḍā was asked about the right of one believer unto another, to which he responded,

"It is the right of the believer that his brother (in faith) carries affection for him in his heart, consoles him with his money, and refrains from showing annoyance with him. If he shows him the least sign of annoyance, there is no association between them. If he tells him, 'You are my enemy,' it's as if one accused the other of faithlessness. If he accused his brother of anything, then faith dissolves in his heart just as salt dissolves in water."[244]

If the issue of rights has all this significance, then its greatest significance is manifest in marital family life. This is because two people must live together for the rest of their lives under one roof. For this reason, a man and woman must have a thorough comprehension of the mutual rights and obligations between them in pursuit of having a calm, loving, peaceful, and safe life.

His Eminence says,

---

[244] *Biḥār al-Anwār*, part 4, page 333.

"Islam defended the rights of women so that women no longer get oppressed, and men cease to consider themselves as rulers over women. In the family, there are boundaries and rights. Men and women both have rights, and these rights were established with great justice and balance.

"As for the things that are being falsely raised in the name of Islam, we neither raise them ourselves nor defend them. What Islam wants are the basics and givens of Islam, which balance the woman and man's rights within the family.

"Emphasis must be given to the responsibility of the man and woman towards each other; each has his own responsibility in creating the family. The happiness of both lies in that.

"Islam stood against the oppression that had befallen women in the age of Jahiliyyah. Islam defined the value and rights of a woman in the fields of morality, thought, Islamic values, politics, and, most importantly, the family. There's no escape for a man and woman from creating the miniature society that is the family. If a family is created in a society which doesn't define values properly, then the family will be the first station in which a woman is oppressed.

"Islamic rulings and teachings in the domain of relationships between a man and woman within the family are very precise. Allah ﷻ stipulated these rulings based on the nature and interests of men and women and the interests of the Islamic community. A man has the right to command his wife and she must obey him in only three situations. I will mention one clearly and disregards the rest. It's his right to prevent his wife from leaving the house without his permission, unless there's a condition in the marriage contract that cancels this right. However, if there was no such condition, then the man has the right to prevent her.

This issue is one of the subtle secrets of the divine decrees. This right was only given to the husband. It wasn't even given to the father; a father doesn't have the right to require his daughter to ask for permission every time she wants to go out. The brother doesn't have that right either in regards to his sister. As for the husband, he has this right over his wife.

"Women certainly have the right to include in the marriage contract conditions that are in their interest. And both men and women must commit to these conditions. That's why it's a whole other case if she included any conditions."²⁴⁵

#87: A Woman is a Sweet Basil

"A lot of men consider the woman to be their servant who has to obey whatever they say without having the right to say no. If she refuses, her husband would get angry with her and address her with rude and harsh words. Some don't stop at this point; they rather transgress it and beat the woman as if she were something even lower! This oppression was rejected by Islam in its greatness for it is nothing short of the oppression committed in the age of Jahiliyyah."

And His Eminence says,

"The Prophet ﷺ says, 'A woman is a sweet basil and not a housekeeper (qahramāna).' The term 'qahramāna' doesn't mean strength and heroism like it does in Persian. It is rather an Arabic word taken from the Persian language. It briefly means the person who handles things. It means that you must not consider the woman to be the person who handles your affairs at home; do not think that you

---
²⁴⁵ *Dawr al-Mar'a fil-Usra*, Markaz al-Imām al-Khumaynī, first floor, 1434 AH – 2003 CE, pages 38-39.

are her superior and that you have delegated the household chores and children to the worker who is the woman.

"No, this isn't the case at all. The right and proper interaction takes into consideration woman's nature. Islam obliged the man to take care of the woman inside the family as he would a flower: 'A woman is a sweet basil.' This is not related to entering political and social fields, acquiring knowledge, and engaging in different social and political confrontations. It is rather related to the family, where a woman is a sweet basil and not a housekeeper. The Prophet's perception disproves those who claim that the woman's duty is restricted to providing services inside the house.

"In the Prophet's opinion, a woman is flower that needs care. One must look at this being of spiritual and physical gentleness through this lens. This is Islam's viewpoint.

"No one has the right to oppress another, force them to do something, or order them around. Some men think that it's the woman's duty to carry out all their work. It's true that when love prevails within the family between a man and woman, each will serve the other out of desire and eagerness. However, the provision of any service out of desire and eagerness differs from considering the woman to be a servant who serves her husband. There's nothing like that in Islam."[246]

#88: A Woman is a Flower, Not a Business Manager

"In our narrations, it is stated that 'a woman is a sweet basil.' A woman is a flower. Now notice how oppressive and wicked a man would be if he treated a flower with harshness or indifference, and wasn't qualified to protect it, Imagine if, for instance, he forced on her more than she can bear. Having excessive expectations of a woman is intrusive and out of place.

"A woman is a sweet basil, and not a housekeeper. *Qahramān* nowadays means business manager. A woman is not your business manager, on whose shoulders you can drop all your lives' burdens then hold her accountable. No, she is a flower in your

---

[246] *Dawr al-Mar'a fil-Usra*, Markaz al-Imām al-Khumaynī, first floor, 1434 AH – 2003 CE, pages 40-41.

hands. Even if she is a scholar or a politician, within the family she is a flower."[247]

Like Partners, Like Friends

"We used to sometimes see men who consider women to be second-class creatures. However, there are no second-class creatures, for they are both the same and have equal rights in life except in the contexts where Allah distinguished between a man and woman. This distinction is in pursuit of serving a particular interest that is neither advantageous for the man nor harmful for the woman. Therefore, they must live at home like partners and friends."[248]

#89: A Man is a Trustee and a Woman is a Sweet Basil

"Islam considers a man to be a trustee[249] and a woman a sweet basil.[250] This is not a transgression against men and women or a violation of their rights. It is rather out of the correct perception of their nature.

---

[247] The Contract Speech dated 28/6/1379 S.H.

[248] The Contract Speech dated 19/3/1372 S.H.

[249] In reference to the noble verse: "Men are the managers of women." See Sūrat al-Nisā', verse 34.

[250] In reference to the well-known narration by Imām 'Alī: "A woman is a sweet basil, and not a housekeeper." See *Biḥār al-Anwār*, part 100, page 253.

"Their balance is equal. Comparing the gentle and beautiful gender, which provides life with tranquility and moral beauty, to the dependable, mobile, protective party who is responsible for management and work, , both scales will be equal. Neither one will outweigh the other."[251]

#90: Exchanging Roles is Prohibited

"Some people take the wrong path, and this isn't restricted to women. Some men also say, 'Let's exchange sides and, accordingly, the roles of men and women.' What will the result be if we do that? We will not gain anything besides mistakes and the destruction of the orchard that was built upon beauty and benevolence. We will reap nothing else. The desired benefits between them will be suspended, indifference will spread within the household, affection in between the man and woman will be lost, and all that love and adoration – which is the basis for everything – will be gone.

"It happens, sometimes, that the man takes on the woman's role in the house, and the latter becomes the absolute ruler. She starts commanding the man: 'do this, don't do that,' and the man yields to her

---

[251] The Contract Speech dated 22/12/1378 S.H.

submissively. A man like that does not qualify to be a woman's refuge, for she needs a strong refuge. Sometimes, the man forces the woman to do certain things such as shopping and dealing with visitors. Why? Because he is occupied and doesn't have the time. Thus, the basis of the matter is if he doesn't have enough time. he would say, 'Now, I have to go to the department, I have to go to work." Thus, the woman must carry out these tasks. He delegates the heavy and boring tasks to the wife, and, of course, she may occupy herself with them for a few days but it's not her primary job."[252]

#91: The Man Must Work
"The Holy Qur'ān says,

❮Men are the managers of women❯[253]

"This means that it is his responsibility to manage the family affairs. A man must work, for he is responsible for the livelihood of the family. And no matter how much wealth the woman owns, it

---

[252] The Contract Speech dated 22/12/1378 S.H.

[253] Sūrat al-Nisā', verse 34.

remains hers, and she doesn't bear the responsibility of the family's livelihood."[254]

#92: Partnership Not Mastery

"The issue is not that the wife must follow her husband in everything, no. there isn't any law that says that in Islam and the Sharia. Allah's saying, ⟨Men are the managers of women⟩ doesn't mean that the wife must follow the man in all affairs. It also lies not in saying, as those who've never seen Europe yet imitate it and want to do worse than it, that all matters are in the woman's hand, and the man must follow her. This is also wrong. Spouses are partners and friends. Sometimes the man overlooks certain faults and other times the woman does. Sometimes one of them compromises in his tastes and desires, and at other times the other person does so they can manage to live together."[255]

#93: The Natural Difference Between Men and Women

"Allah made women gentle. A woman, compared to a man, can be represented by big thick fingers that can pull rocks from underneath the ground. If such

---

[254] The Contract Speech dated 28/6/1397 S.H.

[255] The Contract Speech dated 19/1/1377 S.H.

fingers were to touch delicate jewelry, it is not known whether they will be able to lift them. However, soft and small fingers that cannot lift the rocks are capable of gathering the pieces of jewelry and gold from the ground. This is the case with men and women. They each have an appropriate responsibility; we cannot determine who carries the heavier one. They both carry heavy responsibilities.

"And since the woman's spirit is gentler, she is in greater need of stability, comfort and recourse to a solid haven. And who is this haven? It's her husband. Allah created them both alongside each other like this."[256]

Two Different Yet Beautiful Perceptions

"A woman's perception of a man is naturally different from a man's perception of a woman, and it should be different. There's no problem in that. A man perceives a woman as the epitome of beauty, gentleness, and sensitivity. He finds her gentle. Islam emphasizes this: 'A woman is a sweet basil; ' that is, a woman is a flower from this viewpoint. She is a delicate being who is a manifestation of beauty,

---

[256] The Contract Speech dated 6/6/1381 S.H.

gentleness, and softness. This is how a man looks at her and her love."[257]

Real and Imaginary Rights

"Rights have a natural source. Real rights are those whose source is natural. Those rights that are mentioned in some places are based on delusions and imagination. The rights that are claimed for men and women must be based on the nature of men and women and appropriate to the nature of their creation."[258]

#94: Taking the Woman's Opinion into Consideration

"Westerners make a huge fuss about the issue of women, and they themselves make mistakes. They say, 'We respect women.' Yes, they respect her in official gatherings, markets, and streets by taking pleasure in her. But are men like that with his wives? How much harm is inflicted on women? How many women are beaten by their husbands? How many catastrophes are taking place inside the house?"[259]

---

[257] The Contract Speech dated 6/6/1381 S.H.

[258] The Contract Speech dated 22/12/1378 S.H.

[259] The Contract Speech dated 28/6/1379 S.H.

"A man mustn't think that because he goes out to the market, interacts with this and that, and brings in some money to the house, that makes him the owner of everything. Half of anything he brings in belongs to the family, and the other half belongs to the woman alone.

"Consideration must be given to the opinion and spiritual needs of the lady of the house. It's not right for a man who used to come back to his parents' house at 10 pm during his celibacy, to keep doing that after he gets married. No! He must be considerate towards his wife."[260]

"In the past, some men used to think that they owned women. No, just as you have rights in your family, so does the woman. You must not use power or force with a woman since she is physically weaker. Some people assume that they must use force, raise their voice, fight, and impose things on their wives."[261]

---

[260] The Contract Speech dated 2/9/1373 S.H.

[261] The Contract Speech dated 11/12/1373 S.H.

A Woman is More Influential

"The woman must understand the man's needs and refrain from pressuring his spirit and doing what may drive him away from life and towards wrongful and illegal behaviors. She must encourage him to endure and resist in the battlefields of life. If his job is demanding in a way that makes him unable to attend to the family's needs, then she mustn't bring it up constantly."[262]

"If the man works in the fields of knowledge or *jihād* or strives to make a living through any job, then the woman must create a supportive environment at home that allows him to go to work with a high morale and get back home eagerly."[263]

"All men like to find tranquility and safety once they enter the house and to feel comfortable there; this is the woman's job."[264]

"A woman has obligations which she must reasonably know. Women must know that if they use reason and intelligence, they will make the man give

---

[262] The Contract Speech dated 10/2/1375 S.H.

[263] The Contract Speech dated 2/9/1373 S.H.

[264] The Contract Speech dated 24/1/1378 S.H.

in. It's true that men are physically stronger. However, Allah created women such that if a man and woman were healthy and normal, and the woman was reasonable, then the person who has greater influence over the other is the woman. This certainly doesn't take place through deception, cunning, and control, but rather through leniency, a warm welcome, cheerfulness, and just a little of endurance. Allah made this endurance within the woman's capacity. A woman must interact accordingly with her husband."[265]

"Some women are demanding with their men, in such a way that they for example say, 'You must buy this, you must prepare that. This person bought this, if I don't buy it I will be humiliated.' She hurts her husband through these words, and this isn't right."[266]

---

[265] The Contract Speech dated 19/3/1372 S.H.

[266] The Contract Speech dated 18/5/1374 S.H.

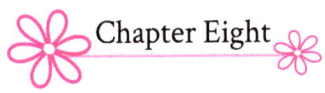
Chapter Eight

Work Division

#95: Work Division

The Guardian of the Muslims, Sayyid Ali Khamenei, says,

"When two people get married and live side by side, there are certain tasks that they share together, such as shouldering the burdens of the family or the diverse cooperation which impacts the progress of the family, for they must cooperate. These things are common between the husband and wife.

"And the ideal situation here is to divide the work. Sometimes it's not feasible to divide it; however, it's better to divide the work in a way that the woman carries out some of the tasks, and the husband completes the rest, as is the case with all other shared tasks or with people who occupy the same position."[267]

"The husband and wife must cooperate within the realm of the family. If the husband is in trouble or going through hardship, then the wife must adapt herself to him. Likewise, if the woman encounters difficulties at work or at home or wherever she is,

---

[267] The Contract Speech dated 22/12/1378 S.H.

then the husband must support her as well. They must consider themselves partners in each other's fate, and they must do it for the sake of Allah."[268]

Cooperation and Reform:

"A man and woman must help one another stay on the right course and straight path. If either of them sees the other do a good deed, he must encourage him and the opposite is true. If they sense a deviation – Allah forbid – then they must work on fixing it, and supporting and encouraging one another to stay on the right path."[269]

"A husband and wife aspire to improve one another, not in a way that makes one of them a master over the other, constantly criticizing, but rather by being like a merciful father and mother."[270]

"The common point between the two spouses in life must be turning to Allah, following the divine commands, and acting upon them. The man and woman much preserve each other on this path, such that if a wife notices that her husband doesn't care

---

[268] The Contract Speech dated 15/1/1378 S.H.

[269] The Contract Speech dated 4/6/1379 S.H.

[270] The Contract Speech dated 22/12/1372 S.H.

about religious matters, she must force him to return to the divine path through wisdom, good manners and the kindness of a woman. And if a husband finds his wife indifferent, then he must take on this task as well. And this is of the essential things in life."[271]

#96: Providing Moral Support

"Cooperation and support don't necessarily lie in someone doing the other person's work; they can rather lie in moral support. Usually, men face more difficult problems in society. Women can make them stronger, relieve them from exhaustion, smile to them and bring them joy. Likewise, if a woman has work outside her house, the husband must provide her with help and support."[272]

"What's meant by cooperation is the spiritual cooperation, such that a woman realizes a man's primary needs, doesn't pressure him ethically, and refrains from doing things that make him abandon his life affairs and lead him – Allah forbid – to taking deviated paths. She must encourage and urge him to persevere and resist in the fields of life.

---

[271] The Contract Speech dated 13/2/1372 S.H.

[272] The Contract Speech dated 15/1/1378 S.H.

"And if his work affects his family conditions, then she must not let him know it. This is what a woman should do. And a man, on his part, is obliged to realize the woman's needs, understand her feelings and never neglect her."[273]

Creating Means, Not Obstacles:

"If a man notices that his wife wants to take positive steps in the path of fulfilling her religious duties, then he must create for her the necessary means rather than putting obstacles in her way. For example, some women want to continue their education or attend religious lectures, or learn the Qurʾān or carry out charitable work. However, their husbands mistreat them by saying, 'We don't have time for this; we got married to live our lives.' They don't allow the woman to do this good deed. There are also some men who want to give enduring charity and contribute to different projects, but their wives don't allow it."[274]

---

[273] The Contract Speech dated 10/2/1375 S.H.

[274] The Contract Speech dated 5/8/1375 S.H.

#97: Women's Work

His Eminence says,

"Some ask us, 'Do you approve of women working?' We say, 'Absolutely.'

We oppose a woman's idleness. A woman must work, and this work is of two types: working at home, and working outside the house. And both are work. If a woman is capable of working outside the house, then she must do it and it's a very good thing, but on the condition that this work – or even work at home – doesn't harm the marital relationship. Some women work from dawn until dusk, then when the men comes home, they're not in the mood to even smile at him. This is bad. The housework must be done, but not to the extent that leads to the destruction of the family."[275]

#98: The Finest Types of Support

"You must be considerate to one another in all circumstances and conditions. Help each other, and be supportive of one another, especially in the field of working for the sake of Allah and in the path of fulfilling one's duty. If the man is the one who's

---

[275] The Contract Speech dated 12/11/1372 S.H.

working for the sake of Allah then the woman must help him, or if the woman is the one who is working for the sake of Allah, then the man must support her. Therefore, whoever is striving in the path of Allah must be supported by the other."[276]

"If a man works in the scholarly field or in the field of activity and struggle (jihād) within the institutions of the Islamic Republic, then the woman must be cooperative so that he can complete his work easily. Likewise, men young men must give their women the opportunity of entering those fields of moral competition, where they can study or participate in social activities if they want to."[277]

"Men and women must seek to guide one another to the path of Allah, support each other in staying on the straight path, and become the manifestation of His saying:

Enjoin one another to [follow] the truth, and enjoin one another to patience[278]

---

[276] The Contract Speech dated 8/3/1381 S.H.

[277] The Contract Speech dated 5/1/1372 S.H.

[278] Sūrat al-Aṣr, verse 3.

This verse is one of the features of Islam and one of the most important characteristics of faith; the husband and wife must always keep it in mind."[279]

"By 'help' we don't mean washing dishes and its likes – of course this is a type of help. What's meant is moral and intellectual support; that is, to support one another in staying firm in the path of Islam and enjoin each other to piety, patience, religiosity. It's to advise one another of chastity, contentment, and asceticism, and to cooperate so they can – if so Allah wills – live in the best way possible."[280]

#99: The Importance of House Work

"The work done by a woman inside the house is not less important – nor less exhausting – than the work done outside; nay, it may rather be more exhausting. A woman needs to strive and make efforts to manage the house, since she is the manager of the house. The mistress of the house is the person under whose supervision, management and administration lies the family. And this is also exhausting and precise work; only feminine skillfulness is capable of attending to

---

[279] The Contract Speech dated 8/5/1375 S.H.

[280] The Contract Speech dated 13/12/1377 S.H.

such work. No man carries out this work with such accuracy."[281]

"Therefore, a woman is not 'idle' inside the house, as some people believe. No! A woman carries out the most numerous, difficult, and crucial tasks inside the house."[282]

"Some people think that assigning housework to women is an offense to women. No, there's no insult in that; for the most important work for a woman is to make daily life run smoothly."[283]

#100: Childcare is a Great Skill

"Some house chores are quite difficult. Raising children is one of those difficult tasks. Any job, and no matter how difficult you imagine it to be, in reality becomes easy when compared to raising children. Childcare is a great art, and no man can carry out this work for even one day. As for women, they do this great work with accuracy, pleasure, and good humor. Allah has placed such power within their instincts.

---

[281] The Contract Speech dated 6/6/1381 S.H.

[282] The Contract Speech dated 18/12/1376 S.H.

[283] The Contract Speech dated 8/3/1381 S.H.

Raising children is, in reality, hard work which exhausts a person and wears them out."[284]

#101: Work-Life Balance

"The youth who work for the sake of Allah must not be hindered by marriage."[285]

"We always advise men not to neglect their homes and lives when they have work. Some leave from the early morning until ten o'clock at night. No! We advise those who can to return to their homes at noon and have lunch with their wives and children, even if it's only for one hour, and then they can go back to work. They can return home early in the evening to sit with their children and really be with them."[286]

Women are Stronger In Multiple Ways

"Those men you see with the body and muscles? All these things are mere appearances. However, mentally and emotionally, women are stronger than men and have a greater capacity for tolerance and problem-solving. This is the nature of women, and

---

[284] The Contract Speech dated 22/8/1384 S.H.

[285] The Contract Speech dated 19/9/1371 S.H.

[286] The Contract Speech dated 18/6/1376 S.H.

this is the case for the majority of women. Certainly, some women may not be like this, but the point is that women are more capable of courteously overcoming depressing things. With a bit of compromise, politeness, and the means available to them, women attend to this role and take the man to wherever he must be, so that life becomes – if so Allah wills – more beautiful."[287]

Lady al-Zahrā', the Role Model:

"You must have all heard about the life of Lady al-Zahrā' in terms of the simplicity of the marriage ceremony, and then the life of that great woman, a life of poverty and asceticism. There was a room and simple bed; she worked inside the house and made her great efforts and showed patience alongside a husband like Imām 'Alī who was occupied with work and activity all his life.

If there was a battle, 'Alī would be at the front lines, and wherever there was important work, 'Alī would at the forefront. They lived together for approximately ten years. Do you notice?

---

[287] The Contract Speech dated 24/1/1378 S.H.

Look at how this young husband managed – within ten years – to carry out his customary duties towards his wife and children.

Lady al-Zahrā' had patience with a life like this, with such poverty and hardship, attending to that great struggle (jihād), and raising such children while making great sacrifices. You've heard about only a few of these sacrifices. All this is an example in life. Thus, our daughters must follow the path of Lady al-Zahrā', and our sons must follow the path of Lady al-Zahrā' and Imām 'Alī."[288]

---

[288] The Contract Speech dated 24/9/1376 S.H.

www.ingramcontent.com/pod-product-compliance
Lightning Source LLC
Chambersburg PA
CBHW061203070526
44579CB00010B/114